S0-ECM-898

GATEWAY
TO ENGLISH

BEYOND
THE
CLASSROOM

Ruth Cathcart • *Michael Strong*

NEWBURY HOUSE PUBLISHERS, INC.
ROWLEY, MASSACHUSETTS 01969
ROWLEY • LONDON • TOKYO
1983

Library of Congress Cataloging in Publication Data

Cathcart, Ruth, 1947–
  Beyond the classroom.

  (The Gateway to English series)
  SUMMARY: A textbook of American language and
culture for people with elementary knowledge of
English. Focuses on such situations as shopping,
looking for an apartment, and applying for a job.
    1. English language--Text-books for foreigners.
2. English language in the United States.
[1. English language--Textbooks for foreigners]
I. Strong, Michael, 1945–   II. Title.
III. Series: Gateway to English series.
PE1128.C445   428.2'4   80-17083
ISBN 0-88377-170-5   Rev.

Book design by Sally Carson

Photographs by David Chase   *Illustrations by Peter Zafris*

NEWBURY HOUSE PUBLISHERS, INC.

Language Science
Language Teaching
Language Learning

ROWLEY, MASSACHUSETTS 01969
ROWLEY • LONDON • TOKYO

First printing: February 1983
Printed in the U.S.A.   5   4   3   2   1

Acknowledgments

2193891

We would like to thank the following people, without whom this book could not have been produced.

John Dennis for lifesaving editorial assistance which was performed with patience, understanding and good humor;

Barry Goward and Timothy White, whose artistry was responsible for most of the ideas behind the drawings, if not the drawings themselves;

Nancy Cedras and Donne Karstens for speedy and error-free typing;

Joanne Dresner, Linda Malila and Tom Nunnelly, who helped field test parts of the book.

To our mothers

Introduction

The design of this book

Beyond the Classroom is an ESL text designed for adult learners at the intermediate level of instruction. The materials and their use are intended for three related but distinct groups:

* "False beginners"—Those students who know the rudiments of English grammar and are beyond beginning literacy.
* Those students who have had a semester or two of ESL instruction (150–300 hours), proceeding from beginners' status.
* High school students who want to integrate their study of English with the study of survival skills, leading to the basic competency examination.

Beyond the Classroom is, in its conceptual design, a survival skills text. In cultural and linguistic terms it provides the following:

* Cultural topics and experience in those aspects of life and language which are central to understanding how things are done in American society.
* Language functions necessary to the communication topics.
* Grammatical structures to increase students' awareness of the new language are graded and spiraled throughout the text.
* Vocabulary and idioms appropriate to the cultural topics presented.
* Exercises in pronunciation, listening and responding that increase recognition and oral production skills.
* Practical tasks that put newly acquired information to work.
* Self-testing sections (quizzes) that allow students to assess their progress and provide a measure of accountability for teachers using the text.

Beyond the Classroom consists of 12 units, each of which is a broad cultural topic. The units/topics are these:

1: Money
2: Looking for an Apartment
3: Furnishing an Apartment
   (Quiz—Topics 1 to 3)
4: Sickness and Injury
5: Transportation Problems
6: The Dentist
   (Quiz—Topics 4 to 6)
7: Applying for a Job
8: Shopping: The Drugstore and the Grocery Store
9: Visiting Friends
   (Quiz—Topics 7 to 9)
10: Travel
11: Clothing
12: On the Phone: Problems with Utilities
   (Quiz—Topics 10 to 12)

v

The table of contents provides a detailed list of linguistic and cognitive features.

Each unit/topic in *Beyond the Classroom* is divided into four parts. Each part consists of this recurrent design:

* An oral/conversational segment, which uses a dialogue followed by pronunciation, vocabulary and idiom notes whenever necessary and appropriate.
* A structure/function segment that provides practice in using patterns from the dialogue and the review of previously presented grammatical features and vocabulary.
* A listening/response segment which also makes use of inferential thinking.
* A task-oriented segment that requires students to apply what they have learned and extend their learning to analogous situations.

Beyond the Classroom was developed for and tested in ESL classes that met five days a week for two hours a day. Four days were used for presentation of the four parts in each unit/topic; the fifth day was used for "wrap-up," review of supplemental (optional) activities of an oral or written type. At the lower (beginning) end of the intermediate level, students sometimes required more time and a slower pace to complete the materials. Students at the middle or high end of the intermediate level were always able to work successfully within the five day module.

Teachers who find themselves working with low intermediate classes will have to decide whether to give more time to the presentation of each unit, or to delete segments of the text in order to complete the material within a given period: i.e., a "session" or a semester. *If at all possible, slowing the pace and allowing more time for each unit would be preferable.* The structures and functions in *Beyond the Classroom* are carefully sequenced and interdependent. Students at this level need practice in oral production and listening—recognition and response. Further, the practical segment that requires problem-solving is a way of integrating and confirming material previously presented. The book also lends itself well to multi-level classes. More advanced students can be paired with less advanced learners for oral practice, since tutoring is known to produce effective learning in the tutor as well as the tutee. At other times students can be divided by ability level and more advanced students can make up new conversations while lower level ones can practice the same material until they are comfortable with it.

The use of this book

The segments of each part of the unit/topic require related but distinct skills. Consequently, teachers may want to emphasize the materials in each segment to a greater or lesser degree, according to the evident needs of their students. Differences in rates of learning or in learning styles of students may constrain or encourage such emphases. The aims of the course and the teachers' styles of presentation may also be contributing factors to variation in procedure. The steps which follow are offered as one effective way of using the materials.

SEGMENT ONE: ORAL/CONVERSATION MATERIAL

Step 1: Preliminary. Each unit/topic presents a "key illustration"—a graphic way of indicating topic, focus and context. As a "warm up" procedure, the teacher may ask the students questions about the illustration: "What is this place? What do you do there, (students' names)? Tell us about it. . . ." If students know very little about "This place," the teacher can answer the questions, of course. The question/answer period may be quite brief and end with a short, simple summary of the information provided: "A bank is a building. People put money in the bank. This money is a deposit. People take money out of the bank. This money is a withdrawal, . . . etc."

Step 2: Listen and Understand. Students close their books and listen as the teacher reads the dialogue twice, at normal conversational speed, with normal intonational contours (that is, without undue emphasis).

Step 3: Comprehension Check. The teacher checks the students' comprehension by asking questions such as: "Who are the people in this conversation? Where are they? What do they want to do, buy, etc.?" The students respond. If they have difficulty, the teacher reads the dialogue again. The students should be encouraged to use the context to work out the meanings of unfamiliar words or phrases.

Step 4: Teacher Explanation. Some students may still be in doubt about the meanings of individual items in the conversation. If so, the teacher may put these items on the board and explain them.

Step 5: Fluency Practice. The teacher reads the first two lines of the conversation, and the students repeat them in chorus. The teacher stays with their practice, working by row and by individual, until most students can say the line fluently. The teacher repeats this procedure until the class has completed the conversation. (In developing fluency, students may need further work with the examples and descriptions in the "pronunciation boxes" following the conversation. This material is not a separate part of the lesson; it is a reminder that certain features of pronunciation may cause difficulty.)

Step 6: Role-Play (1). The teacher takes the part of Speaker 1. The students take the part of Speaker 2.

Step 7: Role-Play (2). The reverse of Step 6.

Step 8: Role-Play (3). The teacher divides the class in two. Half the class takes the role of Speaker 1. The other half, Speaker 2.

Step 9: Paired Practice. Students work in pairs. The teacher monitors and facilitates as the students practice.

SEGMENT TWO: STRUCTURAL/FUNCTIONAL MATERIAL

The Structures and Functions segment contains review material from previous lessons and new material derived from the conversations. Each exercise has a stated focus and brief, clear examples. The teacher may need to read the explanations to the students and even restate the explanations in other ways. The connection between the explanation (the "rule" or description) and the examples must be clearly understood. These procedures may be used for practice.

Step 1—Further Explanation. (Books closed) The teacher writes the example on the board and explains it to the students. The students practice making sentences like those in the example:

I had some money, but he didn't have any.

I had some money, but she _____ .

_____ had some _____ , but my sister _____ .

Step 2—Oral Practice. The teacher may read the exercise one item at a time and call on individual students to respond appropriately. This activity may also be done by pairs of students working orally with their books open. One student takes the part of 1 or reads the stimulus phrase. The other student plays 2 (if the exercise is in dialogue form), or gives the answer (if the exercise is in stimulus/answer form). The teacher then adds some more items, using the students' names, and familiar objects.

Step 3—Extensions. When each exercise has been completed orally, the students relate the patterns to their own lives. This activity may be teacher-directed or done by students in pairs. The students ask each other what they did yesterday, or they ask questions with *did,* such as: "Did you see *Casablanca*?" Then, "Why?" or "Why not?" so that they can practice answering with *because* or *any*: e.g., "I didn't see it because I didn't have any money."

Step 4—Written Work. (Books open) After the oral work is finished, the students can open their books and write the exercises. This could also be done as homework.

SEGMENT THREE: LISTENING/RESPONSE MATERIAL

During the past decade, studies in sociolinguistics have shown the importance of *register* in speech; that is, the ways in which setting and role influence the language we use when we speak to one another. **What do you say?** provides students an opportunity to make inferences about who is speaking through matching up a group of utterances with various speakers. The basic questions implied here are these: Who might have said this? Why do you think so? Variations on this procedure ask students to answer questions like these: How would you describe this speaker? (e.g., as chatty, polite, threatening, etc.), Where might this conversation have taken place? (e.g., a hotel desk, a travel agency, the immigration office, etc.). Finally, students are required to *generate* appropriate responses after being given a context (setting and circumstance) and a stimulus.

What do you hear? provides practice in listening. Students need to develop skill in figuring out natural language for themselves. Although the exercises in **What do you hear?** vary from lesson to lesson, they are based on two principles:

* Students at this level need to develop the ability to understand numbers when they are interspersed in ordinary conversation.
* Students at this level need to understand the form and content of spoken discourse.

What do you hear? requires students to listen and respond in a variety of ways to spoken and taped material. These exercises are graded for difficulty and for the complexity of the tasks to be performed.

SEGMENT FOUR: APPLICATION MATERIAL

This segment, which is called **Put it to work**, involves some real-life activity related to the topic of the unit. Some activities are written, e.g., filling out a lease, completing an application form, etc. Some involve spoken English, for instance, suggestions for follow-up activities such as discussions or contact assignments. The reading and writing exercises in this section develop the students' ability to understand the language of forms and documents. This language is more complex than the language in the rest of the lesson. The teacher should explain the meaning of unknown expressions and words, and discuss how to use the documents. The students are not expected to gain active knowledge of all the vocabulary or to use it in their own conversation or writing. They are expected to gain a passive knowledge of the language presented. The aim of these activities is to help students adjust to and feel more comfortable with the red tape that is part of life in the United States.

The Self-Testing Materials appear at the end of units 3, 6, 9, and 12. They are not intended to be complete reviews of grammar, vocabulary and usage. They are selective in what they test. Two types of questions/problems are used: multiple choice and completion, thereby requiring information-retrieval and problem-solving of the students. The Self-Testing segment is designed as an achievement test, but it is possible to find diagnostic value in it, as well. Teachers may wish to augment the testing material, using the same design.

Contents

xvi

BEYOND
THE
CLASSROOM

TOPIC 1

Money

Part 1

Conversation

1: Hi. Guess what just happened at the bank!
2: What?
1: I found a wallet with $300 in it.
2: Did you keep it?
1: No. I turned it in.
2: Why did you do that?
1: Because I felt sorry for the owner.

Vocabulary and Idiom Notes

Just = recently, not long ago
To turn something in = to give it to a manager or some other official person
To feel sorry for = to understand someone's feelings; to feel sad about someone's bad luck

Structures and functions

FOCUS: Review of past tense in affirmative and negative statements and in questions

Examples:

Affirmative	*Negative*	*Question*
I found a wallet.	I didn't find a wallet.	Did you find a wallet?
I cashed a check.	I didn't cash a check.	Did you cash a check?
I had a driver's license.	I didn't have a driver's license.	Did you have a driver's license?

2

Instruction: Practice the past tense in questions and answers using the verbs given. Work in pairs. One student asks the question and the other answers.

Example: *Gò:*   Did you go to the bank?
                    No, but I went to the store.

(a) *go* _____ ?

_____

(b) *get* _____ ?

_____

(c) *write* _____ ?

_____

(d) *read* _____ ?

_____

(e) *finish* _____ ?

_____

FOCUS: Negative answer with *because*

Example: *Cash a check.* Did you cash a check?
                    No, because I didn't have any ID.

Instruction: One student asks a question. The other student gives a negative answer with *because*.

(a) 1: *Watch TV.* _____ ?

      2: No, _____

(b) 1: *Finish the work* _____ ?

      2: No, _____

(c) 1: *Get a good grade* _____ ?

      2: No, _____

(d) 1: *Walk to school* _____ ?

      2: No, _____

(e) 1: *Call the office* _____ ?

      2: No, _____

3

What do you hear?

1. The teacher will read the passage *In the U.S.A.* (Appendix 1). Mark the form of the verb that you hear.

   (a) came   come   coming
   (b) studying   study   studied
   (c) looking   looks   looked
   (d) tell   told   tells
   (e) get   gets   got
   (f) didn't have   don't have   doesn't have
   (g) went   want   wants
   (h) open   opened   opens

2. The teacher will read the same passage again. Write the word that comes before and after the following words.

   (a) _____ United _____

   (b) _____ wanted _____

   (c) _____ find _____

   (d) _____ me _____

   (e) _____ job _____

   (f) _____ have _____

   (g) _____ bank _____

Put it to work

1. Discuss: (a) If you found a wallet would you turn it in? Why or why not?
   (b) Do you carry a lot of money in your wallet?
   (c) What do you think if someone leaves a bag on a table and it is stolen?

2. Go to a bank and ask how to open an account and how to cash a check. Look at the forms and brochures on the tables. Bring some to class and discuss what they are for.

4

Part 2

Conversation

Customer: Excuse me, I'd like to cash my paycheck.
Teller: Did you endorse it?
Customer: Pardon?
Teller: Did you write your name on the back?
Customer: No. Could I borrow your pen?
Teller: Here you are.
Customer: Thanks a lot.

Pronunciation

Notice that I'd like to becomes *I'd liketa*.

(a)   I'd like to cash my paycheck.
(b)   I'd like to use that pen.
(c)   I'd like to go there tomorrow.

Vocabulary and Idiom Notes

Customer = someone who uses the services of a
              bank or store
Teller = a bank clerk
Endorse a check = sign your name on the back of
              the check

Structures and functions

FOCUS: Use of *polite forms: I'd like to . . . I'd like a . . .*

Explanation: When we wish to request a service politely, we use the words *I'd like to . . .* or *I'd like a . . . please.* This is what we might say in a bank:

Examples: I'd like to cash a check, please.
            I'd like a deposit slip, please.

Instruction: Request services politely, using *I'd like a, I'd like to* in the following situations:

(a)   In a restaurant

_____

(b)   In a travel agency

_____

(c)   In a hotel

_____

(d)   In a bank

_____

(e)   In a gas station

_____

FOCUS: Use of polite forms: *Can* or *could* in requests

Explanation: When we ask a favor, we use *can* or *could* to be polite. *Could* is slightly more polite than *can.*

Examples: Can I leave this here?
            Can I use your phone?

(Notice that *can* and *could* are used for asking a *favor,* whereas *I'd like to* is used to request a service when you expect to get what you want.)

Instruction: Make polite requests using *Can I* or *Could I:*

(a)   In a bar

_____

(b) To your landlord

_____

(c) On a bus

_____

(d) In a bank

_____

(e) At a party

_____

FOCUS: Polite forms with *can, could,* and *would* and "you"

Explanation: When making a polite request with the pronoun "you," we can use *can, could,* or *would.*

Examples: Can you open the window, please? Sure . . .
Could you please open the door? Sure . . .
Would you please open this?

(Notice that some verbs take "me" and others do not.)

Examples: Can you *help me*?
Could you *tell me* the time?

Instruction: Make requests and answers like the examples.

(a) At a party

_____

_____

(b) In a store

_____

_____

(c) In a class

_____

_____

What do you say?

Here is a list of requests and a list of speakers and hearers. Put the requests with the different speakers and say why you think they go together. Which are more polite and which are more impolite or informal?

(a) Excuse me, I'd like to borrow this book, please. Thank you. _____

(b) Could I borrow this book, please, Mr. Wong? Thank you very much. _____

(c) Hey, I'm gunna borrow this book, OK? Thanks. _____

(d) I wanna book. Pleeeeeeese! _____

(e) Give me that book *right now*. _____

(1) student to teacher   (4) mother to small child
(2) adult to librarian   (5) small child to mother
(3) sister to brother

What do you hear?

1. The teacher will read some numbers between 1 and 10. Write them in digits (e.g., 8, 9, 4).

_____ _____ _____ _____ _____ _____ _____

2. The teacher will read some more numbers. Now write them in words (e.g., three, seven, two)

_____ _____ _____

_____ _____ _____

3. Now you will hear some numbers between 11 and 20. Write them in digits.

_____ _____ _____ _____ _____ _____ _____

4. Now you will hear some more numbers between 11 and 20. Write them in words.

_____ _____ _____

_____ _____ _____

(See Appendix 2 for the spelling of the number words.)

Put it to work

Do *Check Writing 1*. The teacher will tell you the names of three people and amounts of money you owe to them. Fill out the three checks correctly.

Check Writing 1

No.

_____ 19___   11-222
                                    333

PAY TO THE ORDER OF _____ $ _____

_____ **DOLLARS**

FIRST AND OCEAN NATIONAL BANK
  NEWBURYPORT, MASS.

_____

⑈033609278⑈ ⑈8821 1764⑈

No.

_____ 19___   11-222
                                    333

PAY TO THE ORDER OF _____ $ _____

_____ **DOLLARS**

FIRST AND OCEAN NATIONAL BANK
  NEWBURYPORT, MASS.

_____

⑈033609278⑈ ⑈8821 1764⑈

No.

_____ 19___   11-222
                                    333

PAY TO THE ORDER OF _____ $ _____

_____ **DOLLARS**

FIRST AND OCEAN NATIONAL BANK
  NEWBURYPORT, MASS.

_____

⑈033609278⑈ ⑈8821 1764⑈

Part 3

Conversation

1: Next, please!
2: I'd like to withdraw $50 from my savings account.
   (1 looks at form.)
1: Okay. You didn't sign the form, did you?
2: Oh, I guess not.
1: Would you please sign it right here?

Vocabulary and Idiom Notes

To withdraw money = to take money out of an
                      account
I guess not = No (unsure); I guess so = Yes (unsure)

Structures and functions

FOCUS: Tag questions with *did*

Explanation: The tag form is affirmative when the main verb is negative. In this form, with falling intonation, the tag expects the answer "no." (The tag question with falling intonation often functions as an accusation.)

Example: 1: You didn't sign the form, did you?
                2: Oh, no, I forgot.

Note: If you have an unexpected answer, it must be stressed more heavily:

              1: You didn't pay your rent, did you?
              2: *Yes, I did.*

Instruction: Ask and answer tag questions in the past tense, expecting the answer "no"; or expressing uncertainty, as in the examples above.

10

(a) Cash a check   1: *You didn't cash a check, did you?*

    2: _yes, I did_

(b) Endorse the check   1: _you didn't endorse the check, did you?_

    2: _____

(c) Withdraw money   1: _____

    2: _____

(d) Open an account   1: _____

    2: _____

(e) (Make up your own)   1: _____

    2: _____

Explanation: The tag form is negative if the main verb is affirmative. In this form, it expects the answer "yes." Again, rising intonation expresses uncertainty, whereas falling intonation may cause the tag to function as an accusation.

Example: 1: You stole my money, didn't you?
                (falling intonation = accusation)
            2: Yes.
    or   2: *No! I did not.*

Example: 1: You signed the form, didn't you?
                (rising intonation = true question)
            2: Yes.

Instruction: Now ask and answer some tag questions expecting the answer "yes" as in the examples above. Work in pairs.

(a) Get a job   1: _____

    2: _____

(b) Write a check   1: _____

    2: _____

(c) (Make up your own)   1: _____

    2: _____

(d) (Make up your own)   1: _____

    2: _____

11

What do you say?

The following people are offering something to drink: friend, wife, stewardess on a plane, host at a party, mother. Which of these offers does each one use? Tell how you make your choices.

(a) Would you like coffee or tea, John? _____

(b) Tea or coffee, sir? _____

(c) Tea or coffee, darling? _____

(d) The drinks are over there. Please help yourself. _____

(e) The drinks are over there. Choose one and don't spill it. _____

   (1) friend   (4) host
   (2) wife   (5) mother
   (3) stewardess

What do you hear?

The teacher will read the passage *In the U.S.A.*

1. Fill in the blanks:

I came to _____ United States two _____ ago. I wanted to

_____ , but I didn't _____ any money. I _____ for a job.

_____ was difficult to _____ one. Everyone told _____ to

study English. About two weeks _____ I got a _____ as a janitor.

_____ Friday I got _____ first check. I _____ have a bank

account, so _____ went to the _____ and opened _____ .

2. Without looking at the passage above, write two or three sentences summarizing it.

_____

_____

_____

_____

_____

3. The teacher will read numbers from 20 to 100. Write them in both digits and in words.

Example: Digits: 21, 35
              Words: Twenty-one. Thirty-five.

Digits _____ _____ _____ _____ _____

         _____ _____ _____ _____ _____

Words _____ _____

        _____ _____

        _____ _____

4. Now you will hear some more numbers between 20 and 100. Write these numbers in words.

_____ _____

_____ _____

_____ _____

Put it to work

1. *Check Writing 2:* Write two checks. You have just bought a television and will write a check to the store. You have also just bought a washing machine, and you will write a second check to another store. Guess at the prices.

Check Writing 2

	No.
_____ 19___	$\frac{11\text{-}222}{333}$

PAY
TO THE
ORDER OF _____ $ _____

_____ DOLLARS

FIRST AND OCEAN NATIONAL BANK
   NEWBURYPORT, MASS.

                                  _____

⑆033609278⑆ ⑈8821 1789⑈

No.

11-222
333

_____ 19 ____

PAY
TO THE
ORDER OF _____ $ _____

_____ DOLLARS

FIRST AND OCEAN NATIONAL BANK

NEWBURYPORT, MASS.

�semicolon033609278⑉ ⑉8821 1769⑉

2.   When you deposit money into a bank account, you fill out a deposit slip. Here is an example of a completed deposit slip.

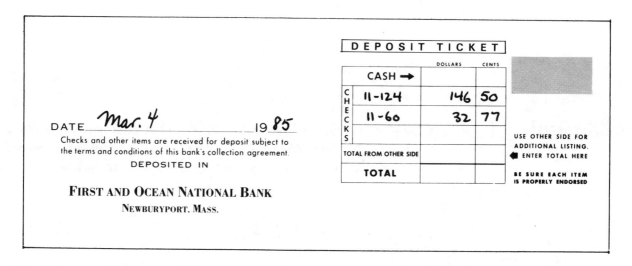

DEPOSIT TICKET		
	DOLLARS	CENTS
CASH ➡		
CHECKS 11-124	146	50
11-60	32	77
TOTAL FROM OTHER SIDE		
TOTAL		

DATE _Mar. 4_ 19 _85_

Checks and other items are received for deposit subject to the terms and conditions of this bank's collection agreement.

DEPOSITED IN

FIRST AND OCEAN NATIONAL BANK

NEWBURYPORT, MASS.

USE OTHER SIDE FOR ADDITIONAL LISTING.
◀ ENTER TOTAL HERE

BE SURE EACH ITEM IS PROPERLY ENDORSED

3.   Fill out the following deposit slip, pretending you received the check for the TV set.

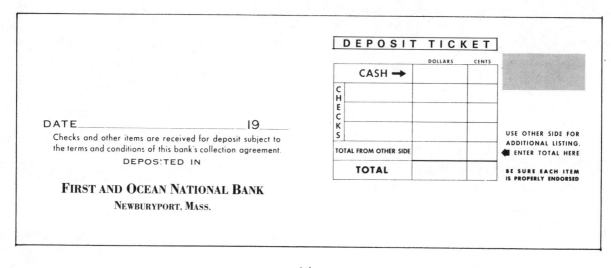

DEPOSIT TICKET		
	DOLLARS	CENTS
CASH ➡		
CHECKS		
TOTAL FROM OTHER SIDE		
TOTAL		

DATE _____ 19 ____

Checks and other items are received for deposit subject to the terms and conditions of this bank's collection agreement.

DEPOSITED IN

FIRST AND OCEAN NATIONAL BANK

NEWBURYPORT, MASS.

USE OTHER SIDE FOR ADDITIONAL LISTING.
◀ ENTER TOTAL HERE

BE SURE EACH ITEM IS PROPERLY ENDORSED

Part 4

Conversation 1   (an emergency)

    1:    Hello, operator, give me the police.
    2:    I'll connect you. Next time, dial 911.

Conversation 2   (another emergency)

    1:    Central Station. Could you hold? . .
           Sorry to keep you waiting.
    2:    I want to report a robbery.
    1:    All right. Your name and address, please.
    2:    Pardon me?
    1:    What is your name?
    2:    Oh. John Mah. Someone stole my wallet. There was $200 in it . . . etc.

Vocabulary and Idiom Notes

Central Station = the name of a police station
Hold = wait (on the telephone)
To connect = to let you talk to a person at another
              number without dialing again
Dial 911 = an emergency number for police and fire

Structures and functions

FOCUS: Asking for repetition with *pardon*

Explanation: *Pardon* or *pardon me* is used to ask someone to repeat what has been said.

Example: 1: I filled in my name and address.
2: Pardon me?
1: I — filled — in — my — name — and — address.

Instruction: Make up conversations like the example where 2 does not understand and 1 repeats. Work in pairs.

(a) 1: _____

2: _____

1: _____

(b) 1: _____

2: _____

1: _____

(c) 1: _____

2: _____

1: _____

(d) 1: _____

2: _____

1: _____

(e) 1: _____

2: _____

1: _____

FOCUS: Emergency calls

The following examples show what you can say in an emergency.

Example: 1: Hello. This is Maria Chavez. I'd like to report a robbery.
2: Yes. Where did this happen? etc.
or 1: Hello. I need an ambulance.
2: What is your name and address? etc.
1: Pardon me? etc.

16

Instruction: Practice reporting emergencies. Work in pairs. One person is the policeman or fireman, and the other reports the emergency.

(a) 1: _____

2: _____

1: _____

2: _____

(b) 1: _____

2: _____

1: _____

(c) 1: _____

2: _____

1: _____

What do you hear?

1. The teacher will read the passage *In the U.S.A.* Write it down on a sheet of paper.

2. The teacher will read some amounts in dollars and cents. Write them in numerals, using the dollar signs and decimals correctly.

   Example: $5.40

   _____ _____ _____ _____ _____

   _____ _____ _____ _____ _____

Put it to work

1. Look up emergency numbers for police, fire, ambulance, and poison center in the phone book. Make up a card to keep by your phone.

2. Discuss theft in America and in your country. Are there a lot of pickpockets, muggers, burglars, armed robbers in your native country? How about here? What should be the punishment for these crimes?

3. Write a short composition about an emergency.

4. Study and fill in the credit application on page 18.

BANK MASTER CHARGE FAST FORM

ABOUT YOU

Full Name _____ Telephone _____

First Name of Spouse _____ Previous Address _____

Address _____ Apt. ___ Single ___ Divorced ___ Married ___

City, State, Zip _____ Social Security _____ Age ___

ABOUT YOUR JOB

Employed by _____ Position _____ How long? _____

Address _____ Previous Employer _____ How long? _____

City, State, Zip _____ Monthly Income _____

ABOUT YOUR HOME

Own ___ Rent ___ Mortgage held by _____

Value of Home _____ Owed _____ Monthly Payment or Rent _____

ABOUT YOUR CREDIT AND FINANCES

Loans From Banks _____ Payment _____ Balance _____

Credit Cards _____ Payment _____ Balance _____

Other Debts _____ Payment _____ Balance _____

The above information is accurate to my knowledge. I authorize the bank to verify the information given above.

Date _____ Applicant's Signature _____

Spouse's Signature _____

Bank Account Numbers

Savings _____ Checking _____

TOPIC 2

Looking for an Apartment

Part 1

Conversation

1: Hello, I'm calling about the apartment you advertised.
2: Sorry, I've already rented it.
1: Oh, well, thanks anyway.
2: I have a house for rent, for $450.
1: No, thanks. That's too expensive for me.

Vocabulary and Idiom Notes

To advertise = to describe something you want to sell, buy, or rent, in a newspaper (or other place)

Thanks anyway = You didn't help me, but thank you for trying

Structures and functions

FOCUS: Present perfect with *already*

Explanation: We use *already* to give an answer that differs from the expectation implied in the question.

Example: Are you looking for an apartment?
No, I've already found one.

Instruction: 1.   Answer these questions, using *already*.

(a)   Does he want some food?

No, he's _____

(b)   Are you going to the post office?

No, I've _____

20

(c) Is she fixing dinner?

No, she's _____

(d) When are you going to see her?

I've _____

(e) What time will you call the agency?

I've _____

(f) Do you want to read this book?

No, I've _____

(g) Is he going to do the washing?

No, he's _____

(h) Are they going to buy a color TV?

No, they've _____

2. Work in pairs. One student asks a question and the other replies with: "*No, I've already . . .*" as in the preceding exercise.

(a) 1: _____

    2: _____

(b) 1: _____

    2: _____

(c) 1: _____

    2: _____

(d) 1: _____

    2: _____

(e) 1: _____

    2: _____

3. Ask about other people in the class.

Example: Is Juan eating now?
No, he's already eaten.

(a) 1: _____

2: _____

(b) 1: _____

2: _____

(c) 1: _____

2: _____

(d) 1: _____

2: _____

(e) 1: _____

2: _____

What do you hear?

1. The teacher will read the passage *A Letter* (Appendix 1). Underline the form of the verb you hear.

(a) have found   haven't found   having found
(b) look   looks   looked
(c) have found   has found   found
(d) shares   is sharing   share
(e) they pay   they paid   they pays
(f) grown   are growing   is growing
(g) I hope   I hoped   I'm hoping

2. When the teacher reads the passage again, write the words that come before and after these:

(a) _____ found _____

(b) _____ far _____

(c) _____ other _____

(d) _____ thirds _____

(e) _____ hoping _____

Put it to work

1. Study the vocabulary and poster chart below.

2. Role-play making calls to ask for different-sized apartments.

   Examples: I'm calling about the three-room flat.
   I'm calling about the house on Sutter Street.
   Do you have a four-room apartment for rent?

1. Highrise building
2. Chimney
3. Attic
4. Curtains
5. Balcony
6. Shades
7. Fire escape
8. Living room
9. Fireplace
10. Hardwood floor
11. Bedroom
12. Rug
13. Kitchen
14. Stove
15. Refrigerator

Part 2

Conversation

1: Hello, I'd like some information about the house for lease.
2: OK, it's a two-bedroom, two-bath unit, all utilities paid.
1: Is it a long-term lease or month-to-month?
2: A six-month lease.
1: Oh, that's too long for me.

Pronunciation

Unstressed prepositions. The vowels in *to* and *for* are usually unstressed or missing.

We say: month-t'-month
and: a house f'rent

(a) He has a house *for* rent.
(b) I gave it *to* Peter.
(c) It's too long *for* me.
(d) I have two cars *to* sell.
(e) He has four houses *for* rent.

Vocabulary and Idiom Notes

Long-term lease = lease for six months, a year, or more
Month-to-month lease = a lease which lasts only one month
Utilities = gas, electricity, and water services

Structures and functions

FOCUS: Number + noun as adjectives

Explanation: When a number and noun are combined to form an adjective, the noun is not pluralized.

Example: Two + bedrooms = a two-bedroom (apartment) (adj)

Instruction: Make sentences using a past tense and an adjective made from these pairs of numbers and nouns:

Example: (Need). Three rooms + apartment
I needed a three-room apartment.

(a) (See) Ten + stories _____

(b) (Pay) Two + months _____

(c) (Want) Four + bedrooms _____

Now begin making up your own sentences with:

(d) 250 + dollars _____

(e) 15 + cents _____

(f) Three + wheels _____

(g) Five + digits _____

FOCUS: *Too*

Explanation: *Too* expresses excess. Notice the differences between *too* and *very*.

Example: I want a 3-month lease. This lease is for six months. That's too long for me.

Instruction: Complete the sentences using *too*.

(a) I have ten people in my family.

A two-room flat is _____

(b) That house costs 750 dollars a month.

It's _____

(c) My son is only twelve years old.

He is _____ to drive a car.

(d) It is very late, and I'm _____ to work any more.

(e) I can't reach the books on the top shelf because I'm _____

_____

What do you say?

These are descriptions of an apartment by different people. Who do you think is talking in each example, and why?

(a) My new apartment is just darling. It's all done in pale blue and has a lovely view of the rose garden.

(b) My apartment is real convenient for downtown; it has a garage and an office where I can work in peace.

(c) I live right near the school. My house has a green front door and I have my own bedroom next to the living room.

(d) This apartment is nearly 700 square feet, with one bedroom, one and a half bath, electric kitchen, and parking space.

    (1) realtor   (3) single man
    (2) single woman   (4) child

What do you hear?

1. The teacher will read the passage *A Letter*. Fill in the blanks.

   I haven't _____ a place to live _____ . I look in the Want Ads every

   day, but _____ is either too far from downtown or _____ expensive.

   My _____ found a great _____ the other day. He's sharing

   _____ two-bedroom house _____ a couple. They pay two-thirds

   _____ the rent, and he _____ one-third. They have _____

   deck and a nice _____ , and they're growing vegetables. _____

   hoping to find something _____ .

2. Don't look at the passage above. Write or say two or three sentences summarizing it (telling what it is about).

   _____

   _____

Put it to work

1. Review the apartment poster. Explain whether you like the rooms in the apartment or not, and explain why, using *too*.

   Example: I don't like the living room because it has too much furniture.

2. Describe your own house or apartment, and your lease:

   Example: It's a two-bedroom apartment. We have a month-to-month lease.

26

3. Begin the Want Ad vocabulary. See the sample Want Ads. Try to read and understand the abbreviations. Work in groups or with the teacher. (Refer to Appendix 4 if necessary.)

APARTMENTS FOR RENT

$110 Sutter studio utils incl single employed no pets 666-0001	$215 unfurn 1 br 1 or 2 pers only AEK hdwd fls 666-0002	$490 Gdn! Statues & fountains! swim pool sauna 2 bedrom 2 bath AEK adult 666-0003
$130 2 rm nr transp yd nudec fee agt 642-9898	$220 2 br frplc patio elev by appt only 642-9899	$650 lux studio view Jacuzzi elev doorman refs req'd 511-8183
$145 2 rms quiet no pets cpts drps stv frig gar nr Med Ctr 511-8181	$260 studio sep kitch month-to-month maid serv sgl only 511-8182	
$185 3 rm gar yd vw fplc mod 919-8537	$350 Breathtaking view huge fplc redec 6 mth lease sunny quiet 919-8538	

Part 3

Conversation

1: Al, have you found an apartment yet?
2: Not yet, I'm still looking.
1: Have you ever shared a house?
2: Yes, but I don't want to share. Other people are always too noisy or too messy for me.

Pronunciation

Notice that *want to* and *want a* both become *wanna* in fast speech. Practice saying affirmative and negative sentences with *want to*.

Examples: I want to go.
I don't want to share.
I want a big apartment.

Vocabulary and Idiom Notes

Share a home = live in a house with someone else
Messy = untidy; disordered; a bit dirty

Structures and functions

FOCUS: Present perfect + *yet*

Explanation: This construction is used in questions when you think that something has happened recently or that it will happen soon.

Example: (Asked at 12 noon) Have you eaten lunch yet?

Explanation: Do not use *yet* if you do not expect the situation to happen.

Incorrect: *Have you gotten sick yet?

(This question can be used only if you know someone has eaten bad food or has been with a sick person.)

Instruction: 1.   Work in pairs. Imagine you are in the following situations. One student asks questions and the other student answers them, as in the following.

Examples: (Looking for an apartment)
Have you called about this apartment yet?
Yes, but the line was busy.

(a) (At the zoo) _____

_____

(b) (In a new city) _____

_____

(c) (At a new school) _____

_____

(d) (At Christmas time) _____

_____

(e) (At housecleaning time) _____

_____

Instruction: 2. Practice describing locations using the map on page 29 asking:

(a) Have you seen the _____ yet?

(b) No. Where is it?

(c) On the corner of _____ and _____ .

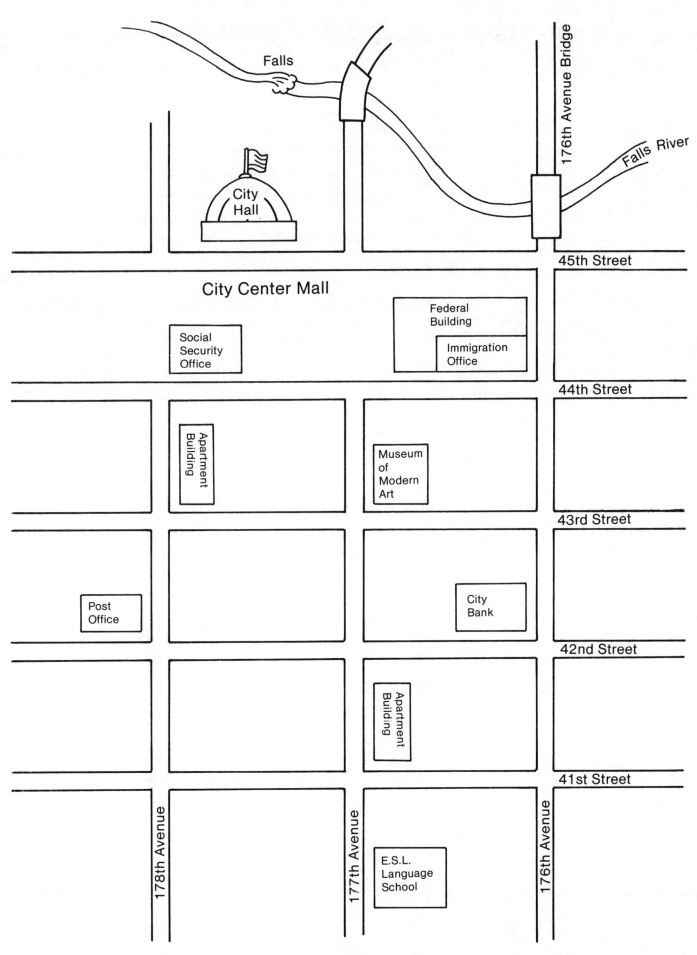

Falls

176th Avenue Bridge

Falls River

City Hall

45th Street

City Center Mall

Federal Building

Social Security Office

Immigration Office

44th Street

Apartment Building

Museum of Modern Art

43rd Street

Post Office

City Bank

42nd Street

Apartment Building

41st Street

178th Avenue

177th Avenue

176th Avenue

E.S.L. Language School

FOCUS: Present perfect + *ever*

Explanation: This construction is used to ask questions when there is only a chance, not an expectation, that the addressee has done the action:

Example: Have you ever skied?
            Have you ever seen the President?
            Incorrect: *Have you ever eaten lunch?

Instruction: One student asks questions about the topics below, and the other student answers.

Example: (Travel)   1: Have you ever gone to San Francisco?
                        2: Yes. I went there last year.

(a) (Food)   1: _____

              2: _____

(b) (Sports) 1: _____

              2: _____

(c) (Illness) 1: _____

              2: _____

(d) (Movies) 1: _____

              2: _____

What do you hear?

The teacher will dictate two-digit numbers to you. Mark the ones that you hear in the order that you hear them. For instance, if you hear 25 as the first number, mark the number 1 beside it. If you hear the number 17 as the second number, mark the number 2 beside that number.

(a)	85	19	71	15	(b)	22	28	82	52
	26	90	11	17		20	62	80	25
	62	59	50	70		12	26	42	75
(c)	32	30	43	93	(d)	18	88	86	65
	23	13	34	39		80	28	60	55
	33	31	73	63		81	68	66	33

Now the teacher will dictate more numbers to you. Write them as you hear them. Watch out for the difference between 18 and 80, etc.

___ ___ ___ ___ ___ ___ ___ ___ ___

___ ___ ___ ___ ___ ___ ___ ___ ___

30

Put it to work   Study the sample lease that follows.

Lease–Rental Agreement

Tenant offers to rent from owner the premises in the city of _____,
County of _____ , at _____ (number and street)
upon the following terms:

TERM: The term shall commence on _____ and continue until
_____ on a month-to-month basis.

RENT: Rent shall be _____ per month, payable in advance, on
the _____ day of each month.

UTILITIES: Tenant shall be responsible for the payment of all utilities except _____
_____ .

USE: The premises shall be used as a residence for not more than _____
adults and _____ children.

PETS: No pets shall be brought on the premises without the written permission of
the owner.

SUBLETTING: Tenant shall not sublet any part of the premises without the written permission of
the owner.

RENT for the period _____ to _____ $_____
Security deposit $_____
Key deposit $_____
Other _____ $_____
TOTAL $_____

The undersigned acknowledges receipt of a copy of this agreement.

Owner _____   date _____

Tenant _____   date _____

Part 4

Conversation

1: Hey! You're as white as a ghost.
2: Yeah, I know. I'm exhausted. I've looked at seven flats in two hours.
1: Well, take it easy, or you'll need a hospital instead of a flat.
2: You're right. Let's go get a beer.

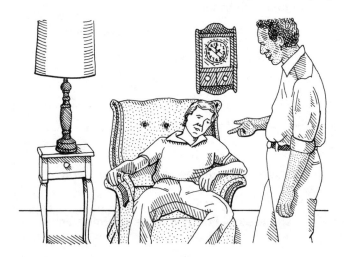

Vocabulary and Idiom Notes

Hey! = a cry of surprise
Exhausted = very tired
Take it easy = relax, slow down
As white as a ghost = white or very pale
Instead of = in place of, as an alternative to

Structures and functions

FOCUS: *Let's go*

Explanation: After *let's go,* a simple verb form is used.

Example: Let's go get a hamburger.
Let's go take some pictures.

Instruction: Make more sentences with *Let's go* +:

(a)   (see) _____

(b)   (find) _____

(c)   (buy) _____

(d)   (make) _____

(e)   (read) _____

FOCUS: *As . . . as*

Explanation: English has certain idioms using *as* _____ *as.*

Example: as white as a ghost, as red as a beet, as blue as the sky, as cold as a fish, as big as a house, etc.

32

Explanation: *As* _____ *as* is also used to compare equal quantities:

Example: My son is as tall as I am.

Instruction: Make sentences comparing equal quantities using:

(a)   As expensive as: _____

(b)   As old as: _____

(c)   As pretty as: _____

(d)   As difficult as: _____

What do you say?

The following questions all ask you to give your address. The form of the address differs according to who is speaking. Read each question and say who you think is asking it, from the choices below. Give reasons for your choice.

(a)   What is your address while you are in the United States?

(b)   Will you have a long way to travel to work each day?

(c)   Are you Miguel Fuerte and do you live at 362 9th St.?

(d)   Oh, I'm from Los Banos too; what street do you live on?

(e)   Street and apartment number. City. State. Zip.

(1)   future employer
(2)   immigration officer
(3)   traffic court judge
(4)   someone at a party
(5)   loan application form

What do you hear?

1.   The teacher will read some sentences with number-adjectives (example: I rented a two-room flat). Write them down.

_____

_____

_____

_____

_____

_____

2. The teacher will dictate digits in the hundreds to you. Mark the ones you hear in the order you hear them.

Example: If you hear 250 as the first digit, mark the number 1 beside it, etc. Try to find the number quickly.

(a)

493	149	639	482
283	745	349	738
893	159	654	473

(b)

616	515	415	414
661	715	617	540
660	670	570	650

(c)

880	980	650	760
780	690	840	550
570	750	860	770

(d)

818	920	880	313
912	215	670	250
212	330	760	101

Put it to work

1. Describe the apartment you lived in before you came here.

2. Get a newspaper and see if you understand the Want Ads. Are the prices the same as in the examples? Do you know the areas of your city where the houses and flats are?

3. Choose an apartment from the Want Ads. Pretend you have rented it. Tell a friend about it.

TOPIC 3

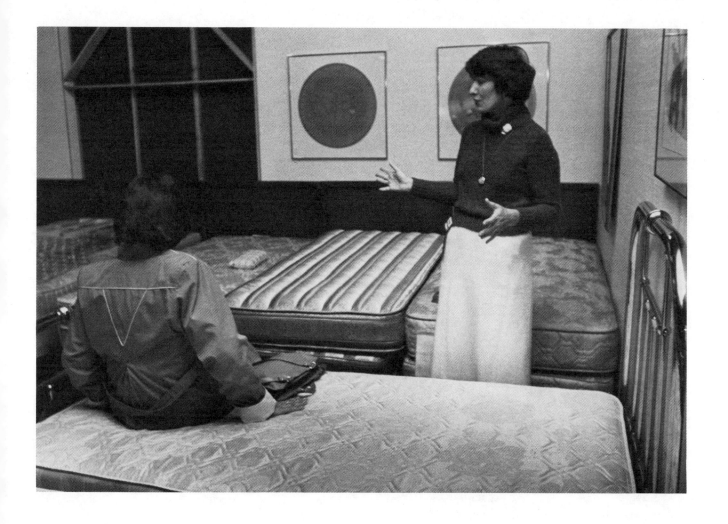

Furnishing an Apartment

Part 1

Conversation 1
   1:   May I help you?
   2:   No, thanks. I'm just looking.

Conversation 2
   1:   Can I help you?
   2:   Yes, I was here the other day. I want to buy a double bed.
   1:   Fine. Do you like this one?
   2:   Yeah, I was looking at it before, but it's so expensive! I can't afford it.
   1:   Well, take your time and look around. I'll be right back.

Pronunciation

th (ð)

the	then	mother	that
other	this	there	father

Notice the difference in pronunciation of *the* if the next word begins with a vowel or consonant.

the dog	the other day
the bed	the ID card
the bank	the account
the driver's license	the exit

Sentences:

(a)   I saw the movie on TV.
(b)   His mother opened the account.
(c)   That's the ID card.
(d)   The teller signed the form.
(e)   I wrote the address over there.

Vocabulary and Idiom Notes

Double bed = a bed for two people
I'm just looking = I don't want any help yet
The other day = a short time, e.g., a few days

Take your time = don't hurry
I can't afford it = I don't have enough money.

I'll be right back = I'll be back very soon

Structures and functions

FOCUS: Past progressive

Explanation: The past progressive is used for an activity which continues for some time in the past. It can be used to contrast a continuing action or event with an action or event which interrupted it.

Example: I was shopping in the supermarket when it began to rain.

Instruction: Tell about some pairs of things that happened at your house last night, using the past progressive.

Example: We *were eating* dinner when my brother *came* in.

(a) _____

(b) _____

(c) _____

(d) _____

(e) _____

FOCUS: Questions and answers using the past progressive

Instruction: Work in pairs. One student asks what the other did at a certain time in the past. The other answers using the past progressive.

Example: 1:   What were you doing at 10:00 P.M. last night?
           2:   I was writing a letter.

(a)   1: _____

      2: _____

(b)   1: _____

      2: _____

(c)   1: _____

      2: _____

(d)   1: _____

      2: _____

FOCUS: Exclamations with *so* plus adjective

Explanation: *So* plus adjective is used to express surprise, wonder, or disbelief.

Examples: This bed is so expensive!
             My apartment is so cold!

Instruction: Make up sentences expressing surprise, wonder, or disbelief about these subjects.

(a)   Someone's new car _____

(b)   An apartment _____

(c)   The weather _____

(d)   A woman _____

(e)   A book _____

What do you hear?

1.   Supply the missing words when the teacher reads the passage *My First Day at Work*.

Well, I'm going to tell _____ about my first day at work _____

Sally's Discount Hardware Store. I got _____ on time (at seven o'clock),

got there at eight, _____ off my coat, and put on _____ name tag.

The boss asked me _____ go around and mark down all _____

prices on TV's. I did that. _____ I sat down and called up _____

wife. I had to tell her _____ pick me up at _____ .

When _____ doors opened, all the sales tags _____ away. I

had to put them _____ quickly. At nine o'clock people began _____

come in. When the customers bought_____ , I had to add up the

_____ and the tax. Sometimes I made _____ , and I had to cross

everything _____ and start again. At five o'clock _____ was worn

out.

2.	The teacher will read the passage again. Fill in the second word of the two-word verbs as you hear them.

(a) got _____

(b) took _____

(c) put _____

(d) mark _____

(e) sat _____

(f) called _____

(g) pick _____

(h) blew _____

(i) put _____

(j) come _____

(k) add _____

(l) cross _____

(m) worn _____

Put it to work

1.	Discuss: What are some of the different features of buying and selling goods in different countries?

What does a seller say when someone comes to a store?
Do you bargain (argue about the price)?
Does a salesperson get more money if he sells more?

2.	Go into a store. Notice what the salesperson says to you. Report back to the class.

Part 2

Conversation

1:	Where were you the day before yesterday? I called and called.
2:	Oh, I went to the sale at Wong's Warehouse.
1:	Were there any bargains?
2:	Sure! Everything was marked down 20 to 50 percent. I bought a washer-dryer.
1:	Sounds good. I might go and take a look.

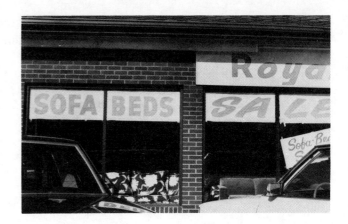

Vocabulary and Idiom Notes

Warehouse = a large building used for storage
To mark down = to lower the price
I called and called = I called again and again.
(Also: I asked and asked = I asked again and again.
BUT: I walked and walked = I walked for a long
   time. I waited and waited = I waited for a
   long time.)

Structures and functions

FOCUS: Expressions of time

Past		Future
Past		*Future*
yesterday	today	tomorrow
the day before yesterday or, two days ago		the day after tomorrow or, two days from now
last week	this week	next week
the week before last or, two weeks ago		the week after next or, two weeks from now

(N.B. Similar expressions can be made with *month* and *year* in place of *week*.)

Instruction: 1. Work in pairs. One student points to a day, a week, or a month, and the other student makes a sentence using one of the above expressions to describe its relationship to the present.

Examples:

JUNE

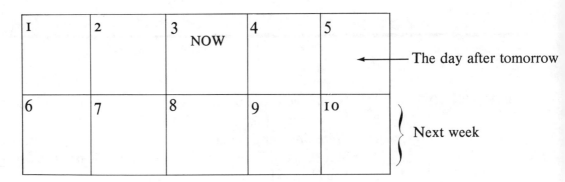

If you want more practice, use a calendar.

2. Use time expressions to answer these questions.

Examples: When was June 19th? It was two weeks ago.
When is your birthday? It is next month.

(1) When is Christmas Day? _____

(b) When is Independence Day? _____

(c) When did school start? _____

(d) When did you arrive in the U.S.A.? _____

(e) When was your last vacation? _____

FOCUS: Use of *might* and present or future

Explanation: Study these examples. Notice that we can express possibility with *maybe* or *might*.

Examples: Maybe I'll go to the movies tonight. =
I might go to the movies tonight.

Maybe he knows the answer. =
He might know the answer.

Instruction: 1. Rewrite the second sentence in each of the following statements, using *might*.

(a) My paycheck arrived today. Maybe I'll buy a color TV.

_____

(b) Here is Wong's Warehouse. Maybe they'll have some bargains.

_____

(c) He is very late. Maybe he'll call soon.

_____

(d) I've lost my checkbook. Maybe the teller has my account number.

_____

(e) I have a cold. Maybe I'll stay home today.

_____

2. Now tell the class what you might do: (a) after school.

_____

(b) when you know English well.

_____

(c) next year.

_____

41

What do you hear?

1. The teacher will read the passage *My First Day at Work* (Appendix 1). Write it down.

2. Study these examples:

1/4	=	one fourth, or one quarter
1/2	=	one half
1/3	=	one third
3/5	=	three fifths
10%	=	ten percent

    Listen as the teacher reads *fractions* and *percents* like those, with numbers up to twenty. Write them here:

    _____ _____ _____ _____

    _____ _____ _____ _____

Put it to work

1. Arithmetic vocabulary: add   subtract   multiply   divide
   + plus   − minus   = equals   ÷ divided by   × times

    Read the following aloud:

    (a) $\begin{array}{r} 1 \\ +3 \\ \hline 4 \end{array}$ (b) $\begin{array}{r} 5 \\ -2 \\ \hline 3 \end{array}$ (c) $\begin{array}{r} 6 \\ \times 2 \\ \hline 12 \end{array}$ (d) $3\overline{)9}$ (e) $1 \times 2 = 2$ (f) $5 \times 1 = 5$

    (g) $8 \div 2 = 4$ (h) $4 - 1 = 3$ (i) $7 + 2 = 9$ (j) $10 \div 5 = 2$

2. Do the following problems:

    (a) What is the total cost of:

    2 towels at $2.99? _____

    3 dishcloths at $1.29? _____

    (b) What is the cost of 5 pairs of gloves at $2.29 per pair?

    _____

    (c) What is the cost of 2 1/2 yards of ribbon at $1.25 per yard?

    _____

    (d) What is the price of a $29.97 mixer if it is on sale for 1/3 off?

    _____

    (e) A man buys two boxes of tissues at 89 cents each. He pays with a ten dollar bill. What is his change? _____

    (f) If extension cords are on sale at two for $3.99, how much is one cord?

    _____

    How much is one extension cord with 5 1/2 percent sales tax added on?

    _____

Part 3

Conversation

1: Excuse me. This blender isn't working. It must be broken.
2: Does it have a guarantee?
1: Yes, I bought it last April, and it has a two-year warranty.
2: Let me see; what's the matter?
1: Well, I turned all the knobs and pushed the buttons, but nothing happened.
2: Why don't you plug it in?
1: Oh dear, how dumb!

Pronunciation

Regular past tenses: Notice that the *ed* past tense may be pronounced like *t* or *d* or *id*. The pronunciation depends on the sound at the end of the verb. (Note: Spelling may change a little.)

Verbs ending in *t/d*	Verbs ending *s/sh/ch* *x/th/f/k* (unvoiced)	Verbs ending in vowels and other consonant sounds
pronounce *id*	pronounce *f*	pronounce *d*
fitted	cashed	turned
wanted	watched	happened

Pronounce these:

(a) started   (b) fixed   (c) used
(d) folded   (e) looked   (f) reserved
(g) loaded   (h) endorsed   (i) paid

(a) We looked at the TV.
(b) The officer folded the papers.
(c) The repair department fixed the vacuum cleaner.
(d) She endorsed the check.
(e) I turned on the washing machine.

Vocabulary and Idiom Notes

Warranty = legal statement or promise that something works well and will be replaced or repaired if it does not
Guarantee = a promise, similar to warranty
Knob = a round handle
Button = a small knob that you push in, usually on TV's, hi-fi's, or cars
To plug in = to connect to the electric outlet
How dumb! = I am so dumb! (*How* used in exclamations instead of questions)
   or: How stupid!
   or: How foolish!
   or: How silly!

Structures and functions

FOCUS: *It must be* + adjective, for expressing conclusions

Explanation: When we use *must be,* we are expressing a conclusion about something based on some evidence.

Example: This TV isn't working. It must be broken.

                                  evidence   conclusion.

Instruction: Now complete these conversations using *It must be . . .* and an adjective. Work in pairs.

(a)   That diamond is very big.

_____

(b)   That man ran 20 miles.

_____

(c)   I can't move my leg.

_____

(d)   My sister has won a beauty contest.

_____

(e)   The hikers started climbing the mountain last week.

_____

FOCUS: Making suggestions

Explanation: "Why don't you . . ." can be used to give someone a suggestion.

Example: 1:   I'm tired.
            2:   Why don't you sit down.

Instruction: Complete these suggestions, beginning with "*Why don't you?*" Work in pairs.

(a)   1:   Brr, I'm very cold.

      2:   "Why _____

(b)   1:   I have no money for the bus.

      2:   "Why _____

(c)   1:   My TV is broken.

      2:   "Why _____

(d)   1:   I hate washing the dishes.

      2:   "Why _____

44

FOCUS: Further work on *it must be* and *why don't you?* etc.

Instruction: Make up short conversations about a customer complaining to a salesman.

(a) 1: _____

2: _____

1: _____

2: _____

(b) 1: _____

2: _____

1: _____

2: _____

(c) 1: _____

2: _____

1: _____

2: _____

**What
do you hear?**

1. The teacher will dictate numbers to you. Write the digits as you hear them.

___ ___ ___ ___ ___ (100's)

___ ___ ___ ___ ___

___ ___ ___ ___ ___ (1000's)

___ ___ ___ ___ ___

2. Write the amounts of money you hear the teacher read.

_____ _____ _____ _____ _____

Put it to work Study the sample warranties which follow.

Part 4

Conversation

1: I saw an ad for a $50 stove.
2: You're kidding. Where?
1: At a garage sale.
2: Hm. That's a good price. Let's go take a look.
1: They have about 200 comic books for sale, too.
2: Oh, now I see why you're interested.

Vocabulary and Idiom Notes

You're kidding = that's impossible (therefore you must be joking)
Garage sale = a sale in a person's garage where they sell their clothes, furniture, etc.

Structures and functions

FOCUS: Expressing uncertainty with *about*

Explanation: *About* may be used if you do not know the exact amount.

Example: How much does it cost?
           It costs about $500. (Maybe $520 or $490)

Instructions: Answer the following questions using *about*.

(a) 1:   How much does a portable TV cost? (*dollars*)

     2:   _____

(b) 1:   How far is it from your home to the school? (*miles*)

     2:   _____

(c) 1:   How much do you weigh? (*pounds*)

     2:   _____

(d) 1:   How much milk do you drink each week? (*pints*)

     2:   _____

(e) 1:   What is the local bus fare? (*cents*)

     2:   _____

Note: It is not polite to ask people the following questions unless they are very young or unless you are very good friends with them:

How old are you?
How much do you weigh?

What do you hear?

The teacher will read sentences from the arithmetic problems. Write them down. Be careful to use the symbols for dollars, percents, and fractions correctly.

(a) _____

(b) _____

(c) _____

(d) _____

(e) _____

47

Put it to work   FOCUS: Asking for information

Instruction: Study the advertisement on page 49. One student makes up questions using the expressions below. Another student answers them.

(a) 1: *How much?* _____

     2: _____

(b) 1: *How many?* _____

     2: _____

(c) 1: *How long?* _____

     2: _____

(d) 1: *What?* _____

     2: _____

(e) 1: *Is?* _____

     2: _____

69.⁷⁵

Dlux radio-cassette
combo!

AM/FM
batteries
extra

9-foot extension cords, plugs,
outlet replacements: your choice,

1.²⁰

Our Price—
11.⁸⁸

Special purchase Sunair Dryer
1000 Watt,
3-speed switch

Compacto travel
alarm clock

Fold-up styles,
simulated leather

7.⁹⁹

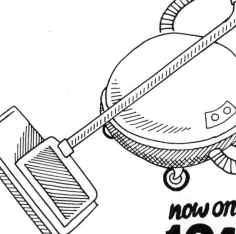

now only—
124.⁹⁵

2-speed Revel
with attachaments
was $229.95

Adjusts for
cleaning ease

599.⁹⁵

Console color TV with
remote control

25" picture, solid state,
Early American cabinet.
Rolling stand, extra.

Quiz, Topics 1 to 3

A. Which one is good English?

1. a. He didn't ate last week.   (Topic 1, Part 1)
   b. He didn't eat last week.
   c. He didn't eats last week.

2. a. I was went to a party last Sunday.   (Topic 1, Part 1)
   b. I went go to a party last Sunday.
   c. I went to a party last Sunday.

3. a. I'd like to buy this TV, please.   (Topic 1, Part 2)
   b. I like to buy this TV, please.
   c. I'd like buy this TV, please.

4. a. I'm already taken a ticket.   (Topic 2, Part 1)
   b. I've already taken a ticket.
   c. I already taken a ticket.

5. a. The customer gave me a twenty-dollar bill.   (Topic 2, Part 2)
   b. The customer gave me a twenty-dollars bill.
   c. The customer gave me twenty-dollars bill.

6. a. Have you see my new car yet?   (Topic 2, Part 3)
   b. Have you saw my new car yet?
   c. Have you seen my new car yet?

7. I'm so tired!   (Topic 2, Part 4)
   a. Well, take it easy. We don't have to hurry.
   b. Well, take easy. We don't have to hurry.
   c. Well, take a easy. We don't have to hurry.

8. a. He such tired!   (Topic 3, Part 1)
   b. He is so tired!
   c. He is a too tired!

9. a. I might to go to a party.   (Topic 2, Part 2)
   b. I might be go to a party.
   c. I might go to a party.

B. Finish these conversations

10. 1: Did you keep _____ ?

    2: No, I _____ . (Topic 1, Part 1)

11. 1: Could I borrow that?

    2: _____ . (Topic 1, Part 2)

12. 1: Oh. Oh. You didn't turn in your application, did you?

    2: _____ . (Topic 1, Part 3)

13. 1: Your name and address, please.

    2: _____ . (Topic 1, Part 4)

14. 1: Excuse me. I'm calling about the house.

    2: _____ . (Topic 2, Part 1)

15. 1: Is it too big for your family?

    2: No, _____ . (Topic 2, Part 2)

16. 1: _____ ?

    2: Not yet. I haven't had the time. (Topic 2, Part 3)

17. 1: _____ ?

    2: It goes down First Avenue. (Topic 2, Part 3)

18. 1: What were you doing at 10:00 last night?

    2: _____ . (Topic 3, Part 1)

19. 1: What are you going to do next year?

    2: I don't know; _____ . (Topic 3, Part 2)

TOPIC 4

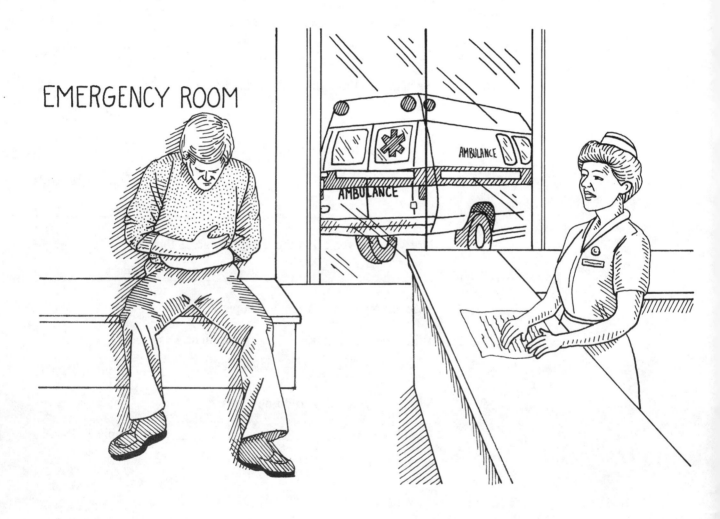

Sickness and Injury

Part 1

Conversation

(At the office)

1: I'm going to go out to lunch now. Where's Alan?

2: He must be at a meeting. He was here at 10:00.

1: He might be sick. He looked kind of pale this morning.

2: Hmm. I have an upset stomach, too. Maybe something's going around.

Pronunciation

Notice

Going to	gunna
Kind of	kinda

Notice also that the *t* in *might* and *must be* is not pronounced in fast speech:

Must be	mus be
Might be	mi' be

Vocabulary and Idiom Notes

Out to lunch = away from the office, having lunch

Kind of = a little bit

Upset stomach = nausea, a sick stomach

Something's going around = A lot of people are getting the same sickness at the same time.

Structures and functions

FOCUS: In Topic 2 you practiced *might* + *verb* and *must be* + *adjective*. Now add *might be*. Pay attention to the differences in meaning and form. When a person uses *must be,* he usually has a reason or evidence, e.g., He must be sick. (I saw him waiting to see the doctor.) *Might be* indicates a guess.

Form: Use an adjective, noun phrase, or *-ing* form after *might be* and *must be.*

Examples: He might be sick.
            He must be a taxi driver.
            She must be walking to school.

Do not use a simple verb form.

Wrong: I might be go to a party.

53

Instruction: Make up responses to the following statements. Remember to use *must be* if there is reason or evidence, and *might be* for a guess.

(a) 1: Look at that woman! She has a huge diamond ring!

    2: _____

(b) 1: I wonder where my sister is.

    2: _____

(c) 1: This fish smells terrible.

    2: _____

(d) 1: I can't remember where I put my watch.

    2: _____

(e) 1: Several students are wearing coats in class.

    2: _____

What do you hear?

1. The teacher will dictate some ordinal numbers to you. Mark the ones you hear from the lists below in the order you hear them. For example, if you hear *5th* as the first number, put the number *1* beside it. If you hear *1st* next, put the number *2* beside it.

(a)

6th	15th	20th	12th
9th	1st	8th	11th
10th	19th	13th	2nd

(b)

3rd	10th	1st	9th
7th	16th	4th	2nd
17th	6th	14th	11th

2. Now the teacher will dictate some more ordinal numbers.

(a) Write them in figures. Example: *5th*

___   ___   ___   ___   ___   ___   ___   ___

(b) Write them in words. Example: *First*

_____ _____ _____

_____ _____ _____

_____ _____ _____

Put it to work   1.   Look at the figures showing body parts on page 56. Learn the vocabulary and review the parts you know which are not labeled (example: nose, mouth).

2.   Practice using body parts vocabulary in sentences like those below. Notice that names for certain parts of the body can be used in certain sentences but not in others.

(a) My _____ hurt/hurts. (throat, back, stomach, kidneys)

(b) I have a pain in my _____ (lungs, ear, liver, stomach, kidney, abdomen).

(c) My child had an operation on his _____ (stomach, knee, throat, gums, etc.).

(d) This medicine is for my _____ infection. (throat, lung, liver, kidney)

throat	large intestine	small intestine
kidneys	heart	stomach
lungs	liver	bladder

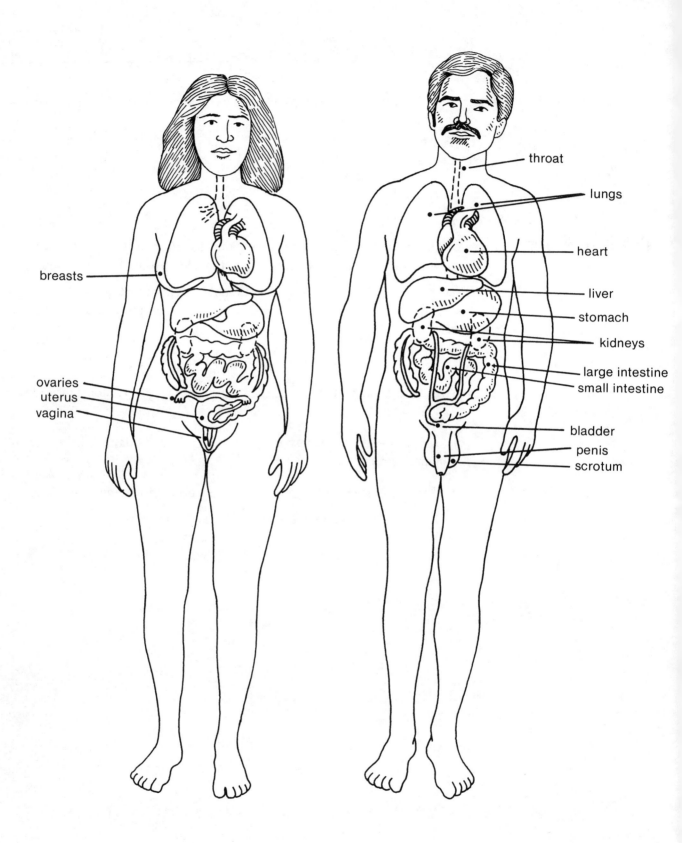

breasts

ovaries
uterus
vagina

throat

lungs

heart

liver

stomach

kidneys

large intestine
small intestine

bladder

penis
scrotum

56

Part 2

Conversation

1: Doctor, what's the matter with me? What's going to happen?
2: That depends on your x-ray.
1: Will I be able to play soccer on the 21st?
2: I don't know yet. If your toe is broken, you won't be able to. If it's sprained, you will.

Vocabulary and Idiom Notes

What's the matter? = What's wrong?
Sprained = when a joint is twisted but no bones are broken
That depends on the x-ray = I will decide when I see the x-ray.

Also:
That depends on the weather = I will decide when I know about the weather.
That depends on John = I will decide when I know what John thinks or wants.

Pronunciation

Th (θ): In Topic 2, you practiced the voiced *th* as in *this*. Now practice the unvoiced *th* as in these words:

bo*th*	ten*th*	for*th*
mon*th*	four*th*	mou*th*
*th*ank you	*th*in	some*th*ing

Sentences:
(a) I have a month-to-month lease.
(b) The bathroom is on the fourth floor.
(c) The thin man bought something.
(d) We both said thank you.
(e) She went to Tenth Street with me.

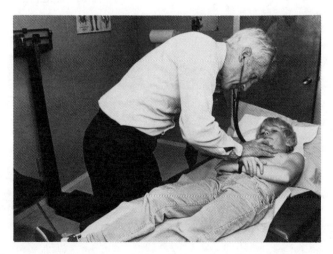

Structures and functions

FOCUS: Future with *will be able to* and *won't be able to*

Explanation: *Will be able to* is used as the future of *can.*

Example: I can't speak English well now, but next year I will be able to.

Instruction: 1. Complete or make up a sentence using *"will be able to."*

   (a)   My little boy can't reach the counter. Next year he _____

   (b)   We can't go swimming in January, but next July we _____

   (c)   I can't walk on my sore foot today _____

   (d)   My baby can't talk now _____

   (e)   My sister is 13 years old, so she can't drive a car _____

2.   Now ask questions using *will be able to.* Example: Will you be able to play tomorrow?

   (a)   I know I can't speak to him today. _____

   _____ tomorrow?

   (b)   Doctor, _____ play tennis _____ ?

   (c)   _____ come to my party?

   (d)   _____ get a job next _____ ?

3.   Now use the negative of *will be able to.* Example: He won't be able to play.

   (a)   I'm sorry. I'm sick and I _____ come to class today.

   (b)   My husband had an operation. He _____ work next week.

   (c)   Next Friday is a holiday. You _____ cash a check.

   (d)   1: I'm going to Miami next week.
         2: Be careful. If you get sick, you _____

   (e)   I'm exhausted so I _____

58

FOCUS: *If* to show future possibility

Explanation: The present tense is used in the *if* clause, and the future tense is used in the main clause.

Example: If I see him, I will (I'll) give him the package.
    or: I'll give him the package if I see him.

Explanation: This construction is often used to place a condition on an answer to a question.

Example: What are you going to do at lunch time?
             I'll go to the bank if I get my paycheck.
    or: If I get my paycheck, I'll go to the bank.

Instruction: Answer these questions. Work in pairs.

(a)   1:   What are you going to do tomorrow afternoon?

     2:   If it rains, I _____

(b)   1:   What are you going to do next quarter?

     2:   If I finish this course, I _____

(c)   1:   What are you going to do in the summer?

     2:   If we have enough money, we _____

(d)   1:   Where are you going to live next year?

     2:   I'll live in the city if I _____

(e)   1:   Who are you going to invite to the party?

     2:   I'll invite Joan if I _____

(f)   1:   When are you leaving for Chicago?

     2:   I'm going to take off at 11:06 if the plane _____

What do you say?

Read these short conversations. Who is speaking? Are they adults or children? Friends? Family? How do you know? Underline the words that tell you.

(a)   1:   Gosh my head hurts.
     2:   Poor thing. Have you taken any aspirin?

(b)   1:   What's the matter sweetheart?
     2:   My tummy hurts.
     1:   Well, let's find something warm for you to drink.

(c) 1: How are you feeling today, Mrs. Garcia?
2: Much better, thank you.
1: That's good. You'll soon be well enough to go home.

What do you hear?

1. The teacher will dictate ordinal numbers between 20th and 100th. Write the digits. Examples: *25th, 59th, 23rd.*

___ ___ ___ ___ ___ ___ ___ ___ ___ ___

2. The teacher will read the passage *The Accident* (Appendix 1). Underline the form of the verb you hear:

(a)	was	wasn't	were
(b)	hitted	hit	hits
(c)	run	running	ran
(d)	got hurt	get hurt	got hurted
(e)	I've been	I been	I'm being
(f)	I never see	I've never seen	I'm never seeing
(g)	must be	must been	must have been
(h)	I'll be able to walk	I'll be able to walk	I'll be able to talk

3. Now fill in the blanks with the correct numbers, as the teacher reads the passage again. Example: Yesterday was the ___16___ th.

(a) It was on _____ st. Street.

(b) _____ cars ran into the wreck.

(c) I've been a reporter for _____ years.

(d) There must be _____ people in the hospital.

(e) I counted _____ broken ribs and about _____ cuts and bruises.

(f) This is how many people got killed _____ .

Put it to work

1. Review the body parts chart on page 56. Practice using body parts in sentences like:

I have trouble with my _____

60

2. Work on useful vocabulary for describing sickness and injury:

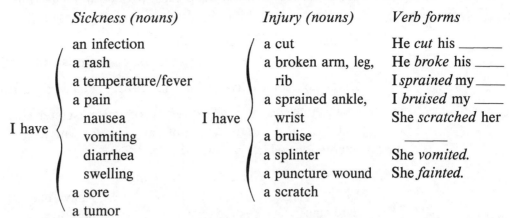

Sickness (nouns)	Injury (nouns)	Verb forms
	a cut	He *cut* his _____
an infection	a broken arm, leg,	He *broke* his ____
a rash	rib	I *sprained* my ____
a temperature/fever	a sprained ankle,	I *bruised* my ____
a pain	wrist	She *scratched* her
I have nausea	I have a bruise	_____
vomiting	a splinter	She *vomited*.
diarrhea	a puncture wound	She *fainted*.
swelling	a scratch	
a sore		
a tumor		

3. Play *What's the matter?*, a game where one person acts out an injury or symptom of a sickness. For example, one student asks, *"What's the matter with me?"* (scratching), and others answer, *"You have a rash"* or (limping) *"You have a sprained ankle."*

Part 3

Conversation

1: I haven't seen you for a long time.
2: I know. I've been on sick leave since April 4th.
1: Oh, that's too bad. Did you have an operation?
2: No, I was in a motorcycle accident.
1: Did anybody else get hurt?
2: No, thank goodness. Just me.

Vocabulary and Idiom Notes

That's too bad = I'm very sorry to hear that.
To have an operation = to be cut open by a doctor
Thank goodness = I'm happy to say
Just = only
Sick leave = time away from work because of
　　　　　illness

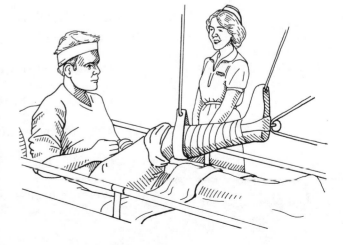

Structures and functions

FOCUS: New uses of the present perfect: *since* and *for*
(See Topic 2 for an introduction to the present perfect tense.)

Explanation: The present perfect is used with *since* when you want to talk about an action or state that began in the past and is still continuing.

Example: I have lived here since 1969 = I came here in 1969 and still live here.

Notice that *since* with an expression of time must refer to the time when the action or state began, not to the *length* of time. Use *for* with lengths of time. Here are some expressions which go with *since* and *for*.

	Since (a certain time)		*For (a length of time)*
I have been here since:	Yesterday	I have been here for:	Two days
	Last night		Several weeks
	Last year		A year
	10:00		An hour
	1970		A long time
	March		Ages
	I was a little boy		
	A week ago		
	Christmas		

Instruction: 1. Practice using *since*. Fill in a time expression.

(a) He has been sick since _____

(b) I have known her since _____

(c) My brother has worked there since _____

(d) Gene has had a checking account since _____

(e) We have been in San Francisco since _____

Note: If you are living in the U.S.A. now, can you say *I have lived in Japan since 1955*? Why or why not?

2. Now do the same sentences, but use *for* instead of *since,* and put in a different time expression.

(a) He has been sick for _____

(b) I have known her for _____

(c) My brother has worked there for _____

(d) Gene has had a checking account for _____

(e) We have been in San Francisco for _____

FOCUS: Negative with *since* and *for*

Explanation: Negative with *since* indicates that the state or action has not occurred between the reference point in the past and the present time.

Examples: I haven't seen him since this morning = I saw him this morning, but I didn't see him in the afternoon or at any other time between morning and now.

I haven't eaten since last night = I ate last night, but I didn't eat this morning or any other time between last night and now.

Negative with *for* indicates the length of time between the last time the action or event occurred and now.

Example: I haven't seen him for nine hours = I saw him nine hours ago, and that was the last time.

Instruction: 1. Finish these sentences:

(a)   I haven't seen my mother since _____

(b)   We haven't gone to a movie since _____

(c)   I haven't eaten Chinese food since _____

(d)   I haven't bought any books since _____

2.   Now do the same sentences again, but use *for* instead of *since*, and put in a different time expression.

(a)   I haven't seen my mother for _____

(b)   We haven't gone to a movie for _____

(c)   I haven't eaten Chinese food for _____

(d)   I haven't bought any books for _____

3.   Mark the sentences which are good English "OK" and rewrite those sentences which are bad English.

(a)   I have studied English since 1970.

_____

(b)   She has lived in Chicago since two months.

_____

(c)   My father has been a bus driver since last July.

_____

(d)   I am in the United States since two years. (two mistakes)

_____

63

(e) We have lived on 21st Street for one month ago.

_____

(f) Kuo hasn't seen a movie since he started work.

_____

(g) My children have been going to school for last year.

_____

4. Finish these sentences about yourself.

(a) I have been a student _____

(b) I have lived in this city _____

(c) I haven't _____ since _____

(d) I have never _____

5. Now work in pairs. One student asks a question and the other answers.

(a) 1: How long have you _____ ?

2: _____

(b) 1: Have you ever _____ ?

2: _____

(c) 1: Have you _____ yet?

2: _____

Put it to work

1. Diseases and injuries and what kind of doctor can help you.

Surgeon   Cardiologist   Urologist
Optometrist   Internist   Gynecologist/Obstetrician
Pediatrician   Veterinarian

Fill in the blanks:

Example: I had a tumor. I went to a surgeon.

I have trouble with my eyes. I need a(n) _____

My child is vomiting. I need a(n) _____

My aunt has trouble with her heart. She needs _____

I have trouble with my lungs. I'll call a(n) _____

My monkey had a tumor. I called a _____

He had trouble with his bladder. He saw a _____

My sister is pregnant. She needs a(n) _____

2. Now describe real problems and tell what kind of doctor is needed.

3. Fill in the Doctor's First Visit Form.

Liz E. Latimer, M.D.
Timothy G. Maynard, M.D.
Ann L. Sidney, M.D.
1520 Pole Street
Modesto, CA 95355

Date_____ Acct. No._____

Patient's name _____
           Last   First   Initial

Address _____
     Number and street   City   State   Zip Code

Phone_____ / Age_____ / Birth date_____

Spouse's name, or parents' (if a minor)_____

Patient's employment_____
  (parent, if a minor)   Occupation   How long   Company and city

Person to be billed _____
         Name and relationship

_____
     Address

Referred by _____

Insurance _____
    Name of Company   Social Security No.   Subscriber

Have you or has anyone in your family ever had:

Problem (check)   Relationship

Fainting spells_____ _____
Diabetes   _____ _____
Tuberculosis _____ _____
Kidney stones_____ _____
Cancer   _____ _____
Asthma   _____ _____
Colitis   _____ _____
Appendicitis _____ _____
Mental illness _____ _____
Mumps   _____ _____
Scarlet fever _____ _____

Part 4

Conversation

Child (in bed): Ohhhh! I think I'm dying. Ohhhh!

Father: Oh, phooey. There's nothing wrong with you. Go to school.

Child: No, *really*! I have a headache and a stomachache.

Father: That's too bad. I wanted to take you to the ball game after school.

Child: Oh, I feel a little better already. I think I'll be able to go.

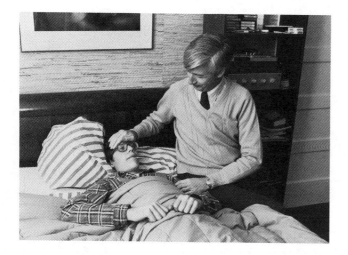

> **Vocabulary and Idiom Notes**
>
> I think I'm dying = I feel sick (exaggeration).
> Phooey = that's silly/stupid

Structures and functions

FOCUS: Discussing illness and injury

Explanation: When someone tells you about an illness or injury, you sympathize or ask for more information.

Examples: Sympathy: 1: I had an operation.
2: Oh that's too bad.

Information: 1: I had an operation.
2: Really? What was the matter?

Instruction: 1. Express sympathy in the following situations:

(a) 1: My son hurt himself playing football.

2: _____

66

(b) 1:   My cousin is very sick.

    2: _____

(c) 1:   I had to go to the dentist this morning.

    2: _____

(d) 1:   Tomorrow I have to get a shot.

    2: _____

2.   Now ask for more information in the same situations.

    Example: 1:   My son hurt himself playing football.
                2:   Oh dear. Did he break a leg?

    (b) _____

    (c) _____

    (d) _____

What do you say?

Formal and informal expressions.

Instruction: Write which words or expressions you would use with the doctor. How about with a friend? Write in "doctor," "friend," or "both."

(a)   Hey! _____

(b)   Gimme something to drink! _____

(c)   I have a problem with my kidneys. _____

(d)   Pardon me? _____

(e)   Excuse me! _____

(f)   So what? _____

(g)   Have a nice day! _____

(h)   You're kidding! _____

(i)   You're welcome! _____

(j)   I appreciate it very much. _____

(k)   Watch it! _____

TOPIC 5

Transportation Problems

Part 1

Conversation

1: Could you take a look at my engine, please? It's making a lot of noise.

2: Sure.

—10 minutes pass—

Well, I think you need a tune-up and a new carburetor.

1: Uh-oh. I hope you can fix it today.

2: I don't know. We're pretty busy.

1: Oh dear, I wish I had a new car instead of this old one.

Pronunciation

A lot of   a lotta   a lodda

Notice that *t* sounds like *d* in the middle of many words. Read the following:

pretty	water	writing
better	bottom	fighting
bottle		
little		

Sentences:

(a) The pretty little girl walked by.
(b) This bottle of water is mine.
(c) He's writing on the bottom of the bottle.
(d) Why are those little boys fighting?
(e) Drink some water, and you'll feel better.

Vocabulary and Idiom Notes

To take a look at = to check

Sure = of course

Carburetor = the device which mixes gas and air in
          a car

Pretty plus adjective (pretty busy) = somewhat

Instead of = in place of

Structures and functions

FOCUS: *Hope* and *Wish*

Explanation: *Hope* is used to indicate wanting something that might be happening or might be true.

Example: *I hope it is sunny* means that I don't know if it is, but I want it to be sunny.

Explanation: Use the present continuous or the verb *to be* after *hope* to express present meaning.

Examples: I hope it *is* warm.
I hope the baby *is sleeping* now.

Instruction: Finish these sentences using *hope* to indicate some things you (or someone else) want(s) to be true.

(a)   I hope my sister _____

(b)   I hope the weather _____

(c)   The mechanic hopes _____

(d)   She hopes the apartment _____

(e)   We hope _____

FOCUS: *Hope* with the future

Explanation: *Hope* can be used with a future tense, too.

Examples: I hope it will rain tonight.
I hope I will be able to play.
I hope you won't be angry.

Instruction: Tell the class a few things you hope for in the future.

(a)   I hope you will _____

(b)   I hope we will _____

(c)   My children hope _____

(d)   I hope my brother _____

(e)   I hope _____ won't _____

What do you say?

Car mechanics talk to different kinds of customers and might say the same thing differently to different people. Tell who you think he's talking to in the following statements. Choose a person from the list below, and say why you make each choice.

(a)   Well sir, you need a new carburetor. Some parts are badly worn. I'll fix it by 5:30 this evening.

(b) The fuel/air mixture is incorrect, two jets are partially blocked, and the idle screw is worn. Needs replacing.

(c) The carb's worthless Bob, you'd better junk it. I'll put a new one in for you.

(d) Tell your dad we have to put a new part in his car because the old one has broken.

(e) See this? No good. Broken. Finished. Put in new one. Understand?

    (1) a friend   (4) a foreigner
    (2) another mechanic (5) a child
    (3) a doctor

What do you hear?

1. The teacher will read the passage *Honest John*; then answer the following questions.

    (a) How many mechanics lived in Reigate? _____

    (b) Did Honest John use new parts to fix cars? _____

    (c) Did his labor cost $25 an hour? _____

    (d) Did Honest John go out of business? _____

    (e) Did the investigators' car need a complete overhaul? _____

    (f) Why did Honest John lose his mechanic's license? _____

2. Now listen to the passage again. This time fill in the articles or adjectives that belong in the following phrases. Sometimes there will be no word to fill the blank.

    (a) _____ very dishonest mechanic   (i) _____ investigators

    (b) _____ only mechanic   (j) _____ small wire

    (c) _____ wheel   (k) _____ Honest John's garage

    (d) _____ new one   (l) He checked _____ car

    (e) _____ new battery   (m) Oh dear, _____ car

    (f) _____ labor   (n) lost _____ mechanic's license

    (g) _____ $25 an hour   (o) _____ man

    (h) _____ people

Put it to work

1. Study the car diagrams and learn the vocabulary. Practice using the names of car parts in sentences like:

    Your _____ doesn't work.

    I'm having trouble with my _____ .

    The _____ is broken.

2. Try to add to the list of car part words by thinking of things which are not included. Look at ads for new cars or think about your own car. Example: "automatic transmission."

    1. Air conditioning switch
    2. Lefthand speaker
    3. Side vent
    4. Steering wheel
    5. Turn signal and headlight control
    6. Flasher control
    7. Horn
    8. Tachometer
    9. Speedometer
    10. Oil gauge
    11. Temperature gauge
    12. Clock
    13. Fuel gauge
    14. Radio buttons
    15. Radio
    16. Cigarette lighter
    17. Ashtray
    18. Gearshift
    19. Glove compartment
    20. Righthand speaker

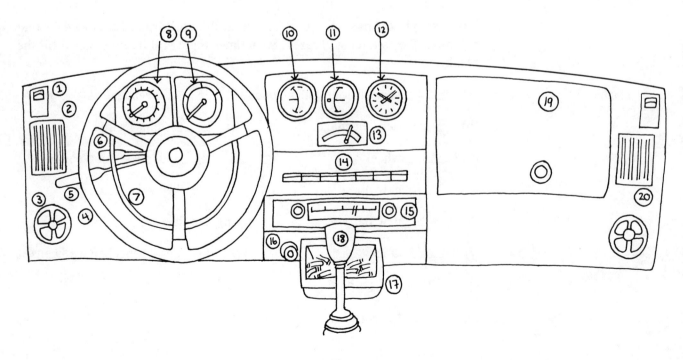

1. Roof
2. Rearview mirror
3. Steering wheel
4. Antenna
5. Hood
6. Headlights
7. Grill
8. Bumper
9. Turn indicators
10. Tires
11. Hubcaps
12. Wheels
13. Door
14. Doorhandle
15. Mirror
16. Seats
17. Safety belt
18. Windshield
19. Windshield wipers
20. Fender
21. Trunk

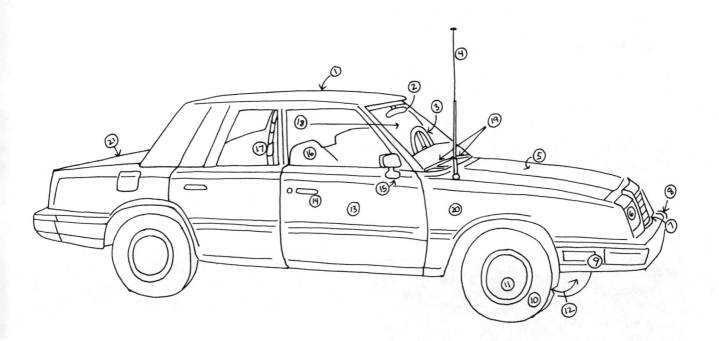

Part 2

Conversation

1: Would you give me a hand?
2: Sure. What's the problem?
1: My engine won't start.
2: Let me see, I used to have some jumper cables.
1: Oh. Do you think the battery's dead?
2: It must be. Your starter doesn't work.
1: Yeah, and my lights don't work, either.

Pronunciation

Used to   usta

Sentences with *used to*:

(a) I used to have a car.
(b) He used to work here.
(c) We used to live in Hong Kong.

Vocabulary and Idiom Notes

Give me a hand = help me
Jumper cables = two heavy wires with clamps at both ends for joining a live battery to a dead battery to start a car.

Structures and functions

FOCUS: *Used to + verb*

Explanation: This construction describes something that took place for a while or repeatedly in the past but has stopped.

Examples: I used to live in Mexico (but now I live in Washington, D.C.)

I used to go to Japan every summer (but now I don't).

I used to be a student (but now I work in a bank).

Instruction: Tell what you did before, using the form *used to + verb*.

(a)   I live in the United States now, but _____

(b)   Now I study English, but _____

(c)   _____ , but now I drive a car.

(d)   _____ , but now I live in an apartment.

(e)   I go to classes once a week, but _____

FOCUS: *Either*

Explanation: 1. When two negative sentences are joined by *and,* or when two negative sentences are joined in conversation, *either* is used after the second one. When the subject is the same for both sentences, it is replaced by a pronoun in the second sentence:

Example: 1:   *Peter* doesn't have a bank account.

2:   *He* doesn't have any credit cards, *either.*

Instruction: Add some information using a pronoun for the subject:

(a)   1:   My sister doesn't speak Spanish.

2:   She _____ , either.

(b)   1:   My car isn't very fast.

2:   _____ , either.

(c)   1:   This apartment isn't very large.

2:   _____ , either.

(d)   1:   Your husband hasn't paid for the utilities this month.

2:   _____ , either.

75

2. When the main verb and its object are the same in both sentences, they may be omitted in the second sentence.

Examples: My sister doesn't play the piano, and my mother doesn't either.
or 1: Your starter doesn't work.
2: Yeah, and my lights don't either.

Instruction: Here are some sentences from conversations. Add some information of your own, using *either* as in the examples above.

(a) 1: My mother doesn't *speak Japanese.*

2: _____ , either.

(b) 1: Your toaster doesn't *work.*

2: _____ , either.

(c) 1: George doesn't *like our new house.*

2: _____ , either.

(d) 1: My Korean friend doesn't *have a driver's license.*

2: _____ , either.

(e) 1: Your wife didn't *endorse that check.*

2: _____ , either.

What do you hear?

1. The teacher will read the passage *Honest John.* Listen carefully and underline which of the verb forms you hear.

(a)	used to	used to be	use to be
(b)	had to	have to	will have to
(c)	charged	charge	charges
(d)	drove	drived	rode
(e)	pull out	pulled out	pulls out
(f)	need	needed	needs

2. Now listen again as the teacher reads the passage, and fill in the missing words.

In Reigate, New York, there used to _____ a very dishonest auto mechanic named _____ John. He was the only mechanic in Reigate. When someone had a flat tire, he _____ to say, "Oh, the wheel is _____ ; you'll have to buy a new _____ ." If a battery died, he used _____ say, "Sorry, you'll have to buy _____ new battery." The sign said that _____ cost $25.00 an hour, but he really charged _____ an hour. Sometimes the parts he _____ in were older than the parts _____ took out. The _____ couldn't do anything about it.

_____ day some investigators from the American Auto Association drove through town. They pulled _____ a small wire from their engine. _____ they went to Honest John's garage. _____ checked their car and said, "Oh, _____ . Your car needs a complete overhaul." A few weeks later, Honest John lost _____ mechanic's license. Another man bought his garage.

Put it to work

1. Describe your car, or a car you would like, to the class. Talk about its size, color, make, engine. Why do/would you like this car?

2. List 5 things that are important to you if you buy a car.

_____

_____

_____

_____

_____

List 2 things you don't like about a car.

_____

_____

3.   Look at some car advertisements in the paper (or commercials on TV). What do the companies say about their cars to make you buy them? List the things the advertisements say are good.

Part 3

Conversation

1:   How much was your new engine?
2:   About $500.
1:   Gee, if I had $500, I'd buy a '55 Chevy.
2:   Old cars are too much trouble. If I were you, I'd take the bus.

Vocabulary and Idiom Notes

Gee = expression of surprise
If I were you = my advice to you is

Structures and functions

FOCUS: Present conditional with *if*

Explanation: In Topic 4, you studied *if* + present tense, which expresses something which might happen. *If* plus *conditional* expresses something which is imagined.

Examples: If + present: If the sun shin*es*, I *will go* to the beach. (It might shine.)

If + conditional: If I *had* a million dollars, I *would go* around the world. (You *don't* have a million.)

Explanation: Notice that the verb in the *if* clause is subjunctive (looks like simple past) and in the main clause it is *conditional* (*would* + simple form).

Instruction: 1. Tell some of the things you would do:

(a) If you spoke English fluently. _____

(b) If you owned a big boat. _____

(c) If you had a rich uncle. _____

(d) If you were President of the United States. _____

(e) If you lost your wallet. _____

2. Now tell some of the things you would not do.

Example: If I spoke English fluently, I would not take this class.

(a) _____

(b) _____

(c) _____

(d) _____

(e) _____

What do you say?

These statements are grammatically correct but are wrong for other reasons. Can you tell why?

(a) Pardon me, would you please give me a hand, Dad?

(b) Hey, Bob, get over here! Could you take a look at my engine, please.

(c) First I want you to fix that Ford, then tune the engine on this car. May I get you some coffee first?

What
do you hear?

This exercise deals with numbers used when we talk about vehicles like cars, trucks, and buses.

Speed is measured in mph (miles per hour); in Europe it is meausred in kilometers per hour (1.6 kilometers = 1 mile). *Tire pressure* is measured in psi (pounds per square inch). Most tire pressures are between 20 and 30 psi. *Length* of cars is measured in feet (ft) and inches (in.). 12 inches = 1 foot. In Europe they use meters plus centimeters (1 meter = 3.3 feet). (Wrench sizes are measured in fractions of an inch.)

The teacher will read the passage *Car Trouble* twice.

1. Answer these questions:

    (a) Is the person's car American or imported? _____

    (b) How fast was she going at the time of the blowout? _____

    (c) Who saw the accident? _____

    (d) How fast did the policeman say she was going? _____

    (e) What are the correct tire pressures? _____

2. The teacher will read the passage once more. Write a brief summary of it.

    _____

    _____

Put it to work

1. Learn to say the names of different makes of cars. Study the Want Ads, page 81. The teacher will write the abbreviations on the board. Try to guess what the full words are.

2. Choose one of the cars. Make up a conversation you might have when you call to get information about it. Work in pairs.

3. Write a want ad for a car you know about or for a car you would like. Show it to other class members and see if they can describe the car.

AUTOS

Buick, '71 Skylark, ex. cond., nu tires, $800, 665-1000.

Camaro, '75, 6 cyl., AM-FM, 20,000 mi., Silver, 886-1120.

Chev. '68 Malibu, 2 Dr., 1 owner, air, nds wk, 556-1033.

Dod. '69 Charger, 4 sp, Ster., 20 mpg, $750.

Ford, '76, Granada, 2 dr, A.T., P.S., P.B. $1300, 522-1073.

Must., '67 Conv., Gd cond., 4 sp., body nds wk., $2700, 662-4211.

VW, '76 Bus, 58K mi, new trans, runs well $3000.

Part 4

Conversation

(At the bus stop)

1: Excuse me. Where does this bus go?

2: Down Main Street, right on 15th, and all the way downtown.

1: How often does it come by?

2: About once every ten minutes. Haven't you ever taken this bus?

1: No. I usually drive to work, but my car broke down yesterday.

2: That's funny. Mine did, too.

Vocabulary and Idiom Notes

That's funny = that seems strange (unusual) to me

81

Structures and functions

FOCUS: *How* + adverb in questions

Examples: How soon will the show start?
How often does the bus come?

Instruction: Ask and answer some questions using *how* + adverb. Work in pairs.

(a) 1: How soon will _____ ?

    2: _____ ?

(b) 1: How soon can _____ ?

    2: _____ ?

(c) 1: How soon _____ ?

    2: _____ ?

(d) 1: How often does _____ ?

    2: _____ ?

(e) 1: How often do _____ ?_____ ?

    2:

FOCUS: *Too*

Explanation: When two affirmative sentences follow each other in conversation, *too* is used at the end of the second sentence to add some information.

Example: *My car* needs a tune-up.
It needs a paint job, too.

Note that the subjects of the two sentences are the same, but the second sentence uses a pronoun.

Instruction: Here are some sentences from conversations. Add some information of your own using *too,* as in the examples above. Use a pronoun in the second sentence.

(a) 1: *That mechanic* fixed your car.

    2: *He* _____ , too.

(b) 1: *This bus* is very fast and comfortable.

    2: It _____ , too.

(c) 1: *Mr. Jones* has two savings accounts.

    2: _____ , too.

(d) 1: *This TV* has a one-year warranty.

    2: _____ , too.

82

(e) 1:   *Jane* wants an apartment with a view.

   2:   _____ , too.

FOCUS: *Do* in responses

Explanation: Note that a form of *do* replaces the verb phrase. The tense stays the same (i.e., past tense *did*; simple present tense *do/does*).

Examples: This car *had* a new paint job.
Yes. That car *did,* too.

Our apartment *has* three bedrooms.
My house *does,* too.

Add some information of your own to the sentences below, changing the subject and using a form of *do* in place of the verb.

(a) 1:   Mr. Simons *went in the hospital* today.

   2:   _____ , too.

(b) 1:   My teacher *speaks three languages fluently.*

   2:   _____ , too.

(c) 1:   I *want to go to a football game.*

   2:   _____ , too.

(d) 1:   Last week the truck drivers *went on strike.*

   2:   _____ , too.

What do you hear?

1.   The teacher will write some abbreviations for heights, speeds, and weights on the board. Tell what they stand for.

2.   Now the teacher will read some speeds and weights. Write them down using the proper abbreviations.

   Examples: Four feet six inches = 4'6"
5 pounds = 5 lb.
25 miles per hour = 25 mph
Kilometers = km.

   _____   _____   _____

   _____   _____   _____

   _____   _____   _____

   _____   _____   _____

3.   Review numbers. The teacher will read cardinal and ordinal numbers, dates, amounts of money, heights, and weights. Write the figures and the symbols that go with them.

Example: (50 mph, $41.00, June 21st)

_____   _____   _____

_____   _____   _____

_____   _____   _____

_____   _____   _____

Put it to work   Bus Routes Conversations

1.   On page 85 you will see the same map you used in Topic 2, Part 3. Now the *bus routes* are filled in. Finish the two-line conversations as in the following example. Work in pairs and use the map to give true answers.

Example: (You are at Bus Stop 4.)

1:   Where does Bus 17 go?
2:   *It goes straight down 176th Avenue, across the bridge.*
1:   How can I get to the Social Security office?
2:   *Take Bus 69 and get off at Stop 3.*

(a)   (At Bus Stop 6)

1:   Where does Bus 29 go?

2:   _____

(b)   (At Bus Stop 5)

1:   Where does Bus 17 go?

2:   _____

(c)   (At Bus Stop 7)

1:   How can I get to Apartment Building X?

2:   _____

(d)   (At Bus Stop 6)

1:   How can I get to the 176th Avenue Bridge?

2:   _____

2.   Now make up your own conversations about the map.

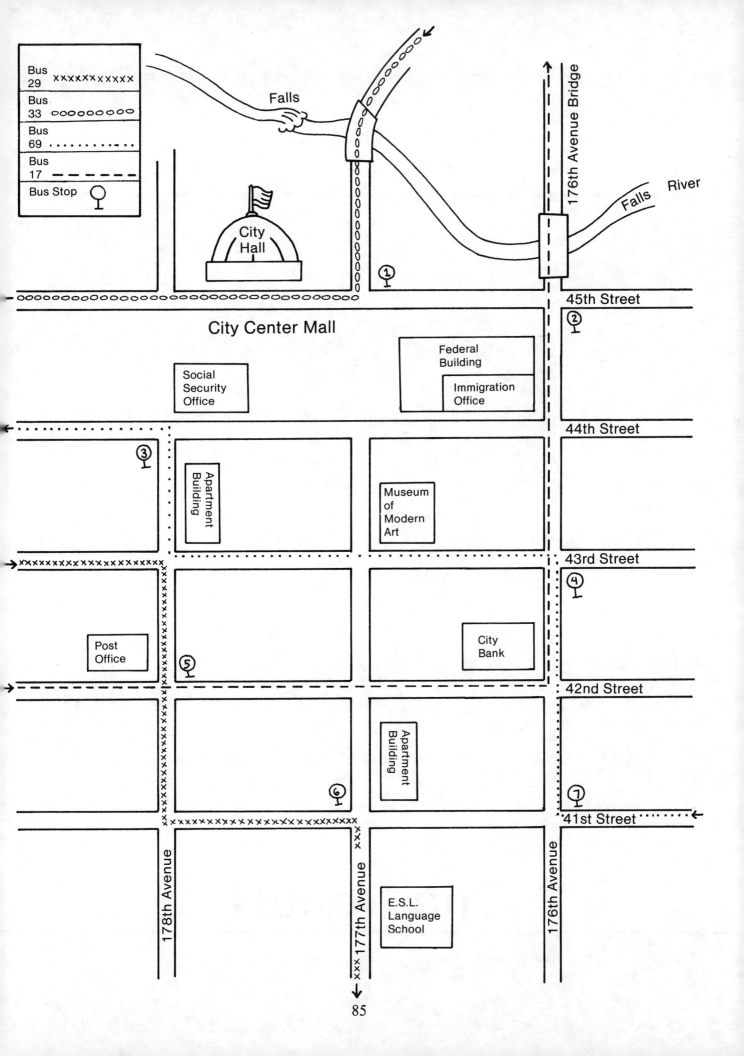

Bus 29 xxxxxxxxxxx
Bus 33 ooooooooo
Bus 69 · · · · · · · ·
Bus 17 — — — —
Bus Stop

Falls

176th Avenue Bridge

Falls River

City Hall

①

45th Street

②

City Center Mall

Federal Building

Immigration Office

Social Security Office

44th Street

③

Apartment Building

Museum of Modern Art

43rd Street

④

Post Office

City Bank

⑤

42nd Street

Apartment Building

⑥

⑦

178th Avenue

177th Avenue

176th Avenue

41st Street

E.S.L. Language School

85

TOPIC 6

The Dentist

Part 1

Conversation

1: Ohhh, I feel terrible.
2: You don't look well. What's the matter?
1: I have a toothache. My whole head hurts.
2: You ought to go to the dentist right away.

Pronunciation

Note: Ought to — odda

Sentences

You ought to go to the dentist.
You ought to get a new car.
He ought to take some medicine.

Structures and functions

FOCUS: Giving advice

Explanation: In Topic 1 you studied *you'd better*. We also use *should* and *ought to* for giving advice.

Example: You should go to the dentist.
You ought to go to the dentist.
You'd better go to the dentist.

Explanation: They all have about the same meaning; however, *should* is used more in writing, and *ought to* and *'d better* are used more in conversation.

Instruction: Work in pairs. One student has a problem. The other student gives him some advice using *should, ought to,* or *you'd better.*

(a) 1: I have a terrible toothache. What should I do?

    2: _____

(b) 1: I don't have any money. What should I do?

    2: _____

(c) 1: I found a ring. What should I do?

    2: _____

(d) 1: My father has a pain in his chest. What should I do?

    2: _____

(e) 1: I missed my bus. What should I do?

    2: _____

FOCUS: Negative advice

Explanation: *Should* and *'d better* take *not* in the negative.

Examples: You shouldn't go there.
              You'd better not go there.

Explanation: Although *ought to* has a negative form (ought not to), it is not often used in conversation.

Instruction: Imagine situations where you give some advice using the negative forms of *should* or *'d better.* Work in pairs. One student makes a statement and the other gives an opinion or advice.

(a) 1: That car is making a lot of noise.

    2: _____

(b) 1: My stomach hurts.

    2: _____

(c) 1: Jan is exhausted.

    2: _____

(d) 1: My neighbors are very messy.

    2: _____

(e) 1: I feel a little sick.

    2: _____

What do you hear?

1. The teacher will read the passage *Dear Mom* twice. Answer the questions:

   (a) Did the patient have a shot? _____

   (b) Was the dentist a man or a woman? _____

   (c) Was the patient a man or a woman? _____

   (d) What did the patient do after she listened to the music?

   _____

2. The teacher will read the same passage again.

   Finish the two-word verbs:

   (a) put _____   (f) turned _____

   (b) came _____   (g) put _____

   (c) cleaning _____   (h) work _____

   (d) put _____   (i) pick _____

   (e) get _____

Part 2

Conversation

1: Doctor, my gums are bleeding.
2: Hmmmm. Yes. They look infected.
1: Do I have to get a shot?
2: I don't think so. It looks like your dentures are rubbing.
1: Do I have to get new ones?
2: No, I think I can adjust them.

89

Pronunciation

Practice:

Have to = hafta

Now read these sentences:

(a) Do I have to get a shot?
(b) Do I have to take the bus?
(c) Do you have to go to the doctor?

Vocabulary and Idiom Notes

Gums = soft flesh around teeth
Infected = red and swollen
Dentures = false teeth
Rubbing = pushing back and forth against something
Adjust = change the position to make something fit better

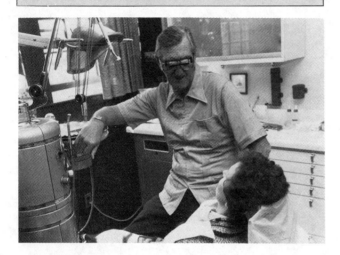

Structures and functions

FOCUS: *Have to* meaning *must* or *is necessary*

Explanation: *Have to* is used more often than *must* in conversation.

Example: 1: Why are you leaving early?
          2: I have to catch a bus.

Instruction: 1. Answer each question using *have to* or *has to*. Work in pairs.

(a) 1: Why is he going into that store?

     2: He _____

(b) 1: Why are you staying at work till 8 p.m.?

     2: _____

(c) 1: Why is she looking at the Want Ads?

     2: _____

(d) 1: Why are you looking up and down the street?

     2: _____

(e) 1: Why do you always eat lunch at 11:00?

     2: _____

2. Ask some questions using *do* or *does* with *have to*.

Example: Do I have to get new dentures?

(a)   Ask the doctor about medicine.

_____ ?

(b)   Ask a car mechanic about your car.

_____ ?

(c)   Ask someone about an apartment.

_____ ?

(d)   Ask a bank teller about an account.

_____ ?

(e)   Ask the dentist about your child.

_____ ?

FOCUS: Verbs of perceiving

Instruction: Practice *it looks like, it sounds like, it feels like,* plus a sentence, as in the following:

Example: The dentist just looked into your mouth.
            He says, "It looks like you have a cavity."

(a)   You just heard a loud crash.

You say, "It sounds like _____ ."

(b)   You just saw a masked man with a gun in the bank.

You say, "It looks like _____ ."

(c)   You just saw two people lying down in the doctor's office.

You say, "_____ ."

(d)   You go outside and feel little drops of water.

You say, "_____ ."

(e)   You hear a siren.

You say, "_____ ."

91

What do you say?

The speakers below are all late after a visit to the dentist. What is the situation in each example? Choose from the list below and tell why you make each choice.

(a) I'm sorry I'm late, Mrs. Evans. I had to go to the dentist. It was an emergency. It won't happen again.

(b) Sorry I'm late, honey. I was at the dentist. Have you been waiting long?

(c) It's not my fault. I had to go to the dentist. You know that.

(d) My excuse is that I was at the dentist. Here's a note from my mother.

(1) Late for school
(2) Late for meeting with girlfriend
(3) Late for work
(4) Late to family dinner

What do you hear?

1. The teacher will read the same passage as in Part 1. Answer the questions using a number.

   (a) What's the date? June _____

   (b) For how long did the patient not go to the dentist? _____ years.

   (c) How many instruments were there? _____

   (d) How long did the patient wait for the dentist? _____ minutes.

   (e) How many x-rays were there? _____

   (f) How many songs did she hear? _____

   (g) How long did she sleep? _____ hour(s)

   (h) How much was the bill? _____

2. Fill in the blanks.

   June 26th

   Dear Mom,

   I put off going to the _____ again. I finally went yesterday after

   _____ years. You must be ashamed of _____ . I was really scared of

   the _____ because I'm allergic to Novocain, as _____ know. When

   I came in, the assistant was cleaning up the instruments. They _____ like

   hundreds of sharp knives. Ugh!

   _____ twenty minutes, the dentist came in. _____ tried to put

   off having my _____ filled, but she didn't let me _____ out of it. The

92

x-rays were _____ . Although I was nervous, the drill didn't _____ too much. Dr. Gore turned up _____ stereo and I could only hear _____ . I put my head back and _____ . I listened to about five songs. I suddenly _____ up three-quarters of an hour later _____ someone said, "Your husband is here _____ pick you up!" What an easy _____ . The $55.00 dental bill was more painful than the filling.

Love,

Jill

Jill

Put it to work Personal letters. Study the letter above. Note the date, greeting, closing, and style of this type of letter.

1. Possible greetings: Write in the blank the people you could be writing to when you use these greetings (a friend, a wife or husband, daughter).

    (a) Dear Sue, _____

    (b) My dearest Sue, _____

    (c) My darling, _____

    (d) My little pumpkin, _____

    (e) Dear John, _____

    Note that we do not use greetings of the forms:

    > To Joe
    > My friend Joe

2. Closings: Write in the blank the people you could be writing to when you use these closings.

    (a) Love, _____

    (b) Love and kisses, _____

    (c) Warmly, _____

    (d) Affectionately, _____

    (e) Your friend, _____

    Note that we do not use *Goodbye* as a closing for a letter.

Part 3

Conversation

1: Have a seat, Mr. Wright. What's the problem?
2: Oh, doctor, I've had a toothache for a month. I need to have my tooth filled.
1: Mmmmmm. It looks like you lost the filling a long time ago. The tooth is decayed.
2: Oh, no. Will I have to have it pulled?
1: I'm afraid so.

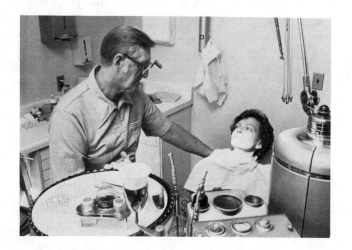

Vocabulary and Idiom Notes

Have a seat = sit down
A filling = metal put in teeth by dentists
Decayed = rotted
I'm afraid so = I'm sorry, yes
(I'm afraid not = I'm sorry, no)

Structures and functions

FOCUS: To have (get) something done; to get another person to do a job for you

Explanation: Form: Use *to have* + noun + past participle

Examples: I want *to have* my tooth filled.
I need *to have* my shoes fixed, too.
I have *to have* my hair cut.

94

Instruction: 1. Answer the following questions using *need to have x done* or *want to have x done.*

    (a)   Why are you going to the dentist?

        _____

    (b)   Why are they waiting at the shoe shop?

        _____

    (c)   Why is he standing in line?

        _____

    (d)   Why is he speaking to the painters?

        _____

    (e)   Why is he going to the beauty parlor?

        _____

2.   Questions: Make present tense questions with *have x done,* as in the following.

    Example: (Present)   Do I need to have my hair cut?

    (a)   Ask a dentist a question.

        _____ ?

    (b)   Ask a doctor a question.

        _____ ?

    (c)   Ask a mechanic a question.

        _____ ?

    (d)   Ask a seamstress a question.

        _____ ?

    (e)   Ask the doctor a question about your friend.

        _____ ?

What do you hear?

Months and years

1. The teacher will read the names of the months. Write them down.

_____ _____ _____ _____

_____ _____ _____ _____

_____ _____ _____

2. Now the teacher will read some years. Write them down in figures.
   Example: 1970, 1965, etc.

_____ _____ _____

_____ _____ _____

_____ _____ _____

_____ _____ _____

_____ _____ _____

Note: The years are read as two numbers. 1970 = nineteen-seventy. The date 1970 is not spoken as one thousand, nine hundred seventy.

Put it to work

Imagine you are writing to a friend or family member. Fill in the date and greeting. Begin writing a letter about a visit to the dentist or the doctor. Use a suitable closing and signature.

Part 4

Conversation

1: How many cavities did you have?
2: Five little ones, but I had them filled.
1: How much did it cost?
2: About $150.
1: I had to pay over $100 for fillings, too.
2: We'd better take care of our teeth. Let's start using dental floss.

Structures and functions

FOCUS: *How much* and *how many.*

Explanation: *Many* is used for countable nouns, and *much* is used for noncountable nouns.

FOCUS: *Had to* for expressing obligations in the past

Explanation: *Had to* is the past tense of *must/ have to/ has to.*

Instruction: 1. Tell how much you or a friend had to pay for things:

Example: (food)   I had to pay over $100 for food.

    (a) (a coat) _____

    (b) (a car) _____

    (c) (an apartment) _____

    (d) (a visit to the doctor) _____

    (e) (a TV) _____

2.   Tell what you had to do:

    (a) yesterday

    _____

    (b) when you came here

    _____

    (c) when you were sick

    _____

**What
do you hear?**

1. Review months and years, if necessary.

2. Americans say "June twelfth" or "May third," but they do not write the "-th" or "-rd" in dates with years:

   Examples: June 12, 1914
                   November 2, 1945
                   July 23, 1947

   However, they do write them in street names:

   Examples: 5th Street
                   33rd Avenue

   Write dates below as the teacher reads them.

   _____   _____

   _____   _____

   _____   _____

   _____   _____

3. Write sentences with dates in them.

   Examples: I went to the dentist on June 4th.
                   I came here in 1970.

   Note: Remember we say *on* a certain day (on June 4) but *in* a year (in 1970).

   _____

   _____

   _____

   _____

Put it to work

1. Finish personal letters.

2. Talk about customs related to the mouth such as:

   The tooth fairy
   Africans filing their teeth as a sign of beauty
   The Vietnamese custom of putting gold in dead people's mouths
   Others?

Quiz, Topics 4 to 6

A. Which one is good English?

1. Joe is absent today.   (Topic 4, Part 1)
   a. He must be go home.
   b. He must go home.
   c. He must be at home.

2. A: My friend died.   (Topic 4, Part 4)
   B: a. Oh. That's too bad.
        b. Oh. That's so bad.
        c. Oh. That's a bad.

3. a. I been here since 1970.   (Topic 4, Part 3)
   b. I've been here since 1970.
   c. I'm here since 1970.

4. a. I wish I had $10,000.   (Topic 5, Part 1)
   b. I wish I'll have $10,000.
   c. I wish I have $10,000.

5. a. I'm used to have a dog.   (Topic 5, Part 2)
   b. I've used to have a dog.
   c. I used to have a dog.

6. If I get a good job,   (Topic 5, Part 3)
   a. I will buy a car.
   b. I would buy a car.
   c. I'd buy a car.

7. A: My sister went to the doctor.   (Topic 5, Part 4)
   B: a. I do, too.
        b. She does, too.
        c. I did, too.

8. a. I look like you have an infection.   (Topic 6, Part 2)
   b. It's look like you have an infection.
   c. It looks like you have an infection.

9. Come in, Mr. Jones.   (Topic 6, Part 3)
   a. Have the seat.
   b. Have a seat.
   c. Have your seat.

10. a. I had to fix my bicycle yesterday.   (Topic 6, Part 4)
    b. I have to fixed my bicycle yesterday.
    c. I didn't had to fix my bicycle yesterday.

99

B. Finish these conversations:

11. 1: _____

    2: Wow! You must be rich!   (Topic 4, Part 1)

12. 1: _____ ?

    2: I think you will.   (Topic 4, Part 2)

13. 1: If it rains, _____

    2: Don't worry. It looks like good weather.   (Topic 4, Part 2)

14. 1: _____

    2: Oh, I'm so sorry.   (Topic 4, Part 4)

15. 1: This is broken. Do you want a new one?

    2: No, I _____   (Topic 5, Part 1)

16. 1: I don't understand this lesson.

    2: _____ either.   (Topic 5, Part 2)

17. 1: I'm so tired.

    2: If I were you, _____   (Topic 5, Part 3)

18. 1: _____

    2: You'd better take a taxi.   (Topic 6, Part 1)

19. 1: Why are you so late?

    2: Sorry. I had to _____   (Topic 6, Part 2)

20. 1: _____ ?

    2: It comes every 10 minutes.   (Topic 5, Part 4)

TOPIC 7

Applying for a Job

Part 1

Conversation

1: Hey, how's it going?

2: Okay. Where have you been? I haven't seen you at The Cat (a bar).

1: I know. I work as a janitor now. I'm on the night shift at the university.

2: That's great. How did you get the job?

1: I applied at the state employment office.

2: I should have done that. I just got a job as a painter, and I don't like it.

Pronunciation

How did you = howdja

How did you get the job?
How did you find my house?
How did you know my name?

Should have = shoulda

I should have done that.
He should have stayed at home.
We should have gone to a movie.

Vocabulary and Idiom Notes

Hey, how's it going? = Hello. How are you? (Very informal among friends)

The night shift = usually from 12:00 midnight to 8:00 a.m.

That's great = very good

Employment office (also called personnel office) = a place where lists of jobs are kept, where people go to get information about jobs

---

Structures and functions

FOCUS: *Should have* (past tense of *should*)

Explanation: Use *should have* to give advice or an opinion to someone who did something wrong in the past.

Example: 1: I didn't pass my test.
2: You *should have* studied harder.

102

Instruction: Use *should have* to give advice or your opinion to speaker A in the following (refer to the example):

(a)　1:　I'm hungry.

　　　2:　_____

(b)　1:　I failed my exam.

　　　2:　_____

(c)　1:　I ran all the way, but I was late.

　　　2:　_____

(d)　1:　I was bored last night.

　　　2:　_____

(e)　1:　My sister couldn't get a job.

　　　2:　_____

FOCUS: Formal and informal greetings

Example:　Here is a list of greetings and responses ranging from formal to informal.
　Levels:　formal, neutral, informal

Formal:
1:　Good morning, Dr. Fillmore.
2:　Good morning.
1:　How are you today?
2:　Very well thank you, how are you?
1:　Fine thank you.

Neutral:
1:　Hi, how are you?
2:　Fine. How are you?
1:　Hello. How are you?
2:　I'm fine. How about you?

Informal:
1:　Hey. What's happening?
2:　Not much.
1:　Hi. How're you doing?
2:　Not bad, how about you?

Instruction: 1. The teacher will say some greetings. For each one, indicate if you could say it to new friends, old friends, the teacher, your boss, or more than one of those.

(a) _____

(b) _____

(c) _____

(d) _____

(e) _____

2. Now work in pairs. One student gives a greeting, and the other answers with an appropriate response. Make the intonation sound natural.

(a) 1: _____

2: _____

(b) 1: _____

2: _____

(c) 1: _____

2: _____

What do you hear?

1. The teacher will read some times of the day. Write the numbers.

Example: 9:00; 9:25

_____   _____   _____   _____   _____

_____   _____   _____   _____   _____

_____   _____   _____   _____   _____

2. Now the teacher will read the times differently. Figure out what numbers represent the time he reads, and write them down.

Examples: A quarter to ten = 9:45
Half past two = 2:30

_____   _____   _____   _____   _____

_____   _____   _____   _____   _____

_____   _____   _____   _____   _____

Put it to work   Complete the job application form on the next two pages.

APPLICATION FOR EMPLOYMENT

PLEASE PRINT

Last Name_____ First Name_____ Middle_____

Maiden Name_____ Name of Spouse_____

Street_____

City_____ State_____ Zip _____

Telephone No. (_____) _____ Social Security No. _____

Previous Address _____

Date of Birth_____ Age _____ Height _____ Weight _____

☐ Single   ☐ Divorced   ☐ Married   ☐ Widowed   Number of Dependents _____ Ages of children _____

Have you ever been employed here before? ☐ yes   ☐ no   If yes, list dates. _____

EDUCATION

School Name and Location _____

Number of yrs. _____ Dates _____ Major Subjects _____

High School___ College___ Other_____

PREVIOUS EMPLOYMENT

Dates	Business name and address	Job Title and Duties	Salary
from:			
to:			
from:			
to:			
from:			
to:			
from:			
to:			

SCHEDULE PREFERRED

☐ Fulltime   ☐ Evenings OK   ☐Part-time   Salary Desired _____

When will you be able to begin work? _____ Any physical defects?_____

Status of Health: _____   If so, describe. _____

Are you a citizen of the U.S.? ☐ yes   ☐ no   Have you ever committed a crime? ☐ yes   ☐ no

If yes, describe. _____

Do you speak/write any foreign languages? _____

Have you ever served in the U.S. Military? ☐ yes ☐ no   Branch: _____ Reserve Status: _____

FOR OFFICE USE ONLY

To the best of my knowledge, all of the above information is true.

Signature _____

Date _____

Part 2

Conversation   1: I'd like to speak to Mr. Chambers, please.
                2: May I ask what it's about?
                1: Tim Allen told me to ask him about a job.
                2: He's at a meeting now. Can I help you?
                1: No, thank you. Perhaps I could make an appointment.

Vocabulary and Idiom Notes

An appointment = an agreement to meet at a certain time

Structures and functions

FOCUS: *Told* + imperative form

Explanation: When someone gives an order (e.g., Get out! Stand up!) and another person reports it, he or she uses *tell* or *told,* a noun or pronoun, and the infinitive.

Example: 1: Get out!
          2: He told me (or, you, him, her, etc.) to get out.

Instruction: Practice finishing these conversations. One person gives an order; the second person does not hear it; the third person reports it, using *told.*

Example: 1: Speak to Mr. Chambers.
          2: What?
          3: He told you to speak to Mr. Chambers.

(a) 1 (to 2): Go to the third street.

     2: Pardon me?

     3: He _____

(b) 1 (to 3): Please stand near the door.

     2: What did he say?

     3: He _____

107

(c) 1 (to 3): Get in line over there.

   2: Pardon?

   3: He _____

(d) 1 (to another person): Be quiet!

   2: What?

   3: She _____

(e) 1 (to another person): Fill out this form.

   2 (to 3): What did she say?

   3: _____

FOCUS: Negative orders

Explanation: Note the example using *not* before the infinitive.

Example: 1: Don't sit there!
          2: What?
          3: He told you not to sit there.

Instruction: Report the following:

(a) 1 (to 2): Don't smoke in the store!

   2: Pardon me?

   3: He _____

(b) 1 (to another person): Don't fill in the last line.

   2: What?

   3: She _____

(c) 1 (to 2): Don't worry!

   2: What?

   3: She _____

(d) 1 (to 3): Don't buy the expensive shoes.

   2: I'm sorry, I didn't understand.

   3: She _____

(e) 1 (to 2 and 3): Don't play in the street!

   2: What, Mommy?

   3: She _____

108

FOCUS: Getting an appointment

Explanation: Sometimes you need to talk to someone, but a secretary won't let you in. You must insist, but be polite, too.

Examples: You: May I speak to Mr. Chambers?
            Secretary: I'm sorry, he's busy now.
                or   he's in a meeting.
                or   he's out now.
            You: Could I make an appointment?
                        Perhaps I could make an appointment.
                        I could wait.
                        Could I wait until he's available?
                        Could I see him later? (or, tomorrow?)

Instruction: One student takes the role of secretary. The other is the applicant. Practice the different ways of talking, as shown in the examples. Do it in front of the class, and pay attention to the tone of voice and body language.

(a)   1: _____

      2: _____

      1: _____

(b)   1: _____

      2: _____

      1: _____

**What
do you say?**

Who are these people talking *to*? How do you know?

(a)   I'd like to find out more about those job openings for a waiter and a gardener.

(b)   Hey, why don't you tell me about the waitress job you mentioned?

(c)   I understand you have a vacancy for a waiter. Can you tell me more about it?

(d)   Be quiet for a minute. I want to hear what Mr. Jones is saying about that job at the restaurant.

          (1)   child   (3)   employment officer
          (2)   friend   (4)   restaurant owner

What do you hear?

Personal Information: The teacher will read some questions from the job application. Write the true answers to the question.

Examples: How tall are you?   Where do you live?
              5'7"   At 525 5th Avenue.

(a) _____

(b) _____

(c) _____

(d) _____

(e) _____

(f) _____

(g) _____

(h) _____

(i) _____

(j) _____

(k) _____

Put it to work

1. Study the Help Wanted section from the Want Ads which follow. The teacher will write abbreviations on the board. Figure out what they mean. Note the vocabulary for different jobs.

2. Make up a phone conversation between you (the applicant) and one of the employers in the Want Ads. Pay attention to polite forms. Work in pairs.

3. Write a want ad for a job you would like. See if other students can figure it out.

HELP WANTED

ACCOUNTING Clerk. Expr'd. Bus. loan application $6/hr. Send resume to AD 3312.

AIRCRAFT Repair Shop Foreman. Min. 3 yrs. exp., $17,000 start. Shift rotates thru holidays and weekends (505) 213-5522

AUTO Mechanic. VW, own tools, salary accd to exper. All benefits. Apply in person. 521 5th St.

BANKING. Teller to $750. 1 yr. exp., 40 hr wk, able to work Sat. Immed. opening. National Bank. 157 So. State St.

COOK, short order, sandwich, hard work, good money. Apply 420 Main.

MAID to work in rest home. M/F. $3.50/hr, reliable. P.O. Box 111.

MAINTENANCE, Hotel, min. 5 yrs. exp. in carpentry, painting, plumbing, all around. Must have wheels and tools. Non-drinker. Ad 2250.

PRINTING, Shop Helper. Learn equip. clean shop, delivery. $3.50 hr. start. 522-0211.

RECEPTIONIST/Typist. Busy phones. Type 50 wpm $800 plus benefits.

WAITRESSES. Must be 21. Apply in person 3–5 p.m. 421 8th Ave.

Part 3

Conversation

1: Who did they hire for that gardening job?
2: I don't know. They wanted someone with experience.
1: I think they hired that guy from Panama.
2: Really? He told me that Mr. Chambers didn't like him.

Vocabulary and Idiom Notes

Hire = to give someone a job
Experience = having had the same kind of job before

Guy = man
Really? = an expression of surprise

111

Structures and functions

FOCUS: *Told + that* for reporting a statement

Explanation: In Part 2 you learned to repeat an order using *told* + infinitive (e.g., he told me to sit down). To report a statement made some time in the past, put a pronoun (me, you, him, her, us, them) after *told*. Then add *that* and the statement. Notice that the present tense is usually changed to past in reported speech.

Examples:
1: What did Mr. Lou say this morning?
2: He *told me* that he had to go to the airport.

1: What did the saleswoman tell her about the dress?
2: She *told her* that it was too big.

Notice that we cannot use "me" with "say."
Incorrect: She said me . . .

Example:
1: I work as a waitress now.
2: What?
3: She said she works as a waitress.

(Note: If the statement is reported right away, we often use *said* or *says.*)

Instruction: Finish the conversations using *told* and adding information of your own.

(a) 1: What did the teller say to you?

    2: _____

(b) 1: What did that woman tell you yesterday?

    2: _____

(c) 1: What did the manager tell him when he went in?

    2: _____

(d) 1: What did the clerk say to the customers?

    2: _____

(e) 1: What did you tell Jane?

    2: _____

FOCUS: Descriptions using *with* or *in*

Explanation: Prepositional phrases are often used to describe people or things. "With" can be used for clothing or personal features. "In" is used only with clothing.

Examples:

A person *with*	The woman *in*
two brothers	the yellow dress
experience	the blue jeans
red hair	high-heeled shoes
a black coat	

112

Instruction: 1. Describe the people sitting near to you, e.g., He's a man with black hair. He's a guy in a red shirt.

(a) _____

(b) _____

(c) _____

(d) _____

2. Describe some people you have seen on the street.

(a) I saw a man in _____

(b) _____

(c) _____

(d) _____

What do you say?

You want to talk to the boss at the Social Security Office. Choose the best way of telling his secretary you want to see him, and say why you chose it. What is wrong with the other examples?

(a) I want to see Mr. Chambers.

(b) Where is Mr. Chambers?

(c) Let me see the boss!

(d) I would like to make an appointment to see Mr. Chambers.

(e) Please take me to Mr. Chambers' office.

(f) Is Chambers here?

What do you hear?

The teacher will read the application letter on page 119 twice.

1. Answer the following questions about the letter.

(a) Who will get the letter? _____

(b) How did the writer know about the job? _____

_____

(c) Does he have experience? _____ How much? _____

(d) How far does he have to go for the interview? _____

113

2. Fill in the prepositions in this passage.

   (a) I saw your advertisement _____ a dress buyer _____ the Want Ads.

   (b) I am intrested _____ working _____ you.

   (c) I have worked _____ the Goodhue Dress Shop _____ a saleslady and part-time buyer _____ two years.

   (d) I can send you a list _____ references.

   (e) I will be _____ Los Angeles _____ January 30th _____ February 5th.

   (f) I would be happy _____ come in _____ an interview at your convenience.

3. Listen as the teacher reads the above passage. Fill in the prepositions again, noting any differences between your version and the teacher's version. Note that more than one preposition is acceptable in some places.

Put it to work

Begin business letters:

1. Talk about the differences in greetings for personal letters and business letters. (Refer to the personal letter, Topic 6.) Notice that business letters begin with the whole address.

2. Look at the business addresses and greetings which follow. Do Parts 1 and 2 with the class. Do Part 3 yourself and talk about it.

What kind of greeting could you use if you have these addresses?

1. You know the company, not the person's name.

   (a) Gemco Manufacturing Co.
       14 W. 5th St.
       New York, NY 10453

       _____ :

   (b) Manager
       Plasco Plate Co.
       21 Slade Ave.
       Boston, MA 02115

       _____ :

2. You know the name of the person you are writing to.

   (a) Mr. John Smith
       Folloly Co.
       149 Geary Blvd.
       San Francisco, CA 94118

       _____ :

   (b) Judith P. Jones
       Director of Personnel
       Playa Filing Company
       1451 20th Ave.
       Chicago, IL 69609

       _____ :

3. Now give the proper greetings for these addresses:

(a) Alice R. Poker
Ballon Toys
13 Oak St.
Biloxi, MS 42200

_____ :

(b) Professor John Blacker
P.O. Box 1477
University of California
Davis, CA 95800

_____ :

(c) Director of Personnel
Okaya Restaurant
2121 First Street
Los Angeles, CA 90056

_____ :

(d) Oakmont Book Co.
140 Harrison Street
Seattle, WA 98103

_____ :

(e) Dr. Maxwell Farley
Exxon Building, Room 41
1500 Embarcadero
Silver Spring, MD 22156

_____ :

(f) Susan Birs
Director of Finance
APX Mortgages
Fox Plaza 147
Bangor, NY 10021

_____ :

Part 4

Conversation

1: Mrs. Wong? Nice to meet you. Come in and have a seat.
2: Thank you.
1: (looking at application) It looks like you have been in the United States for two years.
2: That's right.
1: When did you start working?
2: About a year ago.
1: Could you tell me about your job?
2: Well, I started as a waitress. Now I'm the head waitress. But sometimes I have to wash dishes, too. It's a small place. . . .

Structures and functions

FOCUS: Introductions

Explanation: There are different ways of introducing people, depending on who they are. Refer to these examples: You are introducing two people to each other. If there is a woman and a man, speak to the woman first. That is, introduce the man *to* the woman.

Example: Mary, this is John Packer. John, this is Mary Meyers.
Mary: Nice to meet you.
John: Nice to meet you.

Instruction: Practice this type of introduction in groups of three.

(a)   1: _____

2: _____

3: _____

(b)   1: _____

2: _____

3: _____

Explanation: If one person is much older or much more important, speak to him or her first.

Example: Joe's father: Mr. Smith, this is my son Joe. Joe, this is Mr. Smith.
Mr. Smith: Hello Joe.
Joe: Nice to meet you, Mr. Smith.
or: How do you do?

Instruction: Practice in groups of three: one student introduces, one is the boss, and the third student is the employee.

(a)   1: _____

2: _____

3: _____

116

(b) 1: _____

    2: _____

    3: _____

Explanation: There are other ways of introducing which give some information about the person.

Examples: 1:   Joe, I'd like you to meet my friend Sue. Sue, this is Joe Allen, my sister's boyfriend.

          2:   Nice to meet you.

or: 1:   Mr. Smith, this is the new typist I told you about.

      2:   Nice to meet you.

or: 1:   Sue, this is our manager, Mr. Smith.

      2:   How do you do?

Explanation: In addition to *Nice to meet you* (which is always O.K.), the answers among friends can be very informal, like "Hi, how are you?" A more formal answer would be "How do you do?" or "I'm very happy to meet you."

Instruction: Make up some conversations at the office and with friends. Use the different ways of introducing:

(a) 1: _____

    2: _____

    3: _____

(b) 1: _____

    2: _____

    3: _____

(c) 1: _____

    2: _____

    3: _____

(d) 1: _____

    2: _____

    3: _____

FOCUS: Introducing yourself

Explanation: If you haven't met someone or you think the person has forgotten your name, introduce yourself. Extend your hand and say:

Example: 1: Hello. I'm Sandro Cuevas.
2: Hi. I remember you. I'm Shirley White.

Instruction: Practice introducing yourself to the people around you.

(a) 1: _____

2: _____

(b) 1: _____

2: _____

(c) 1: _____

2: _____

Explanation: If you want the conversation to go on, you can add some information.

Example: 1: Hello, I'm Jin Ho. We met at the Shafers' house last month.
2: Oh yes, I remember.

or: 1: Hello. I'm Jin Ho. I go to school with your brother.
2: Hi. How do you like it there?

Instruction: Make up some self-introductions which add some information.

(a) 1: _____

2: _____

(b) 1: _____

2: _____

(c) 1: _____

2: _____

(d) 1: _____

2: _____

What do you hear?

The teacher will dictate the whole application letter. Write it down. Pay attention to the form; i.e., do the date, the greeting, and the spacing. Use a whole sheet of paper.

Put it to work
1. Write an application letter for one of the jobs from the Want Ads. Use real names, dates, etc.

2. Practice or write interview conversations for some of the jobs in the Want Ads.

3448 Main Street
San Francisco, CA
94108

January 25, 1980

Mr. Joe Alpo
Personnel Director
Wang Ho Clothing Co.
2100 Sutter Street
Los Angeles, CA 95837

Dr. Mr. Alpo:

I saw your advertisement for a dress buyer in the *San Francisco Chronicle* Want Ads (Jan. 20, 1980) and I am very interested in working with you. I have worked for the Goodhue Dress Shop as a saleslady and part-time buyer for two years. I can send you a list of references if you request them.

I will be in Los Angeles from January 30th to February 5th, and I would be happy to come in for an interview at your convenience. Thank you very much for considering my application.

Very truly yours,

Sally Wong

Sally Wong

TOPIC 8

Shopping: The Drugstore and the Grocery Store

Part 1

Conversation

1: This is a prescription for painkillers. Can you fill it right now?

2: Well, let's see. I don't have this brand, but I have a better one. I'll have to call the doctor.

1: How long will it take?

2: If he's available, it will only take me forty minutes.

1: Can't I have it sooner? I have to go to work.

Pronunciation

Practice *l*:

I'll	letter	hello
tell	like	Alice
will	look	fillings

Read:

(a) I'll say hello to Alice.

(b) Did you tell her about the letter?

(c) I don't like to have fillings in my teeth.

(d) Will you look at my throat?

(e) When will you sell it?

Vocabulary and Idiom Notes

Prescription = an order the doctor writes for medicine. The patient takes it to the pharmacy to get the medicine

Painkillers = medicine to stop pain

Brand = a name which identifies the makers of a product or their trade name

Pharmacy = a store or part of a store where prescriptions are sold

Drugstore = a store which has a pharmacy but also may sell other items such as soap, toys, and hardware

Structures and functions

FOCUS: Review of comparatives and superlatives

Explanation: There are irregular forms:

good	better	best
many	more	most
bad	worse	worst
little	less	least (amount)

Explanation: There are regular forms for words of one syllable, and two-syllable words ending in *y* or in syllabic */l/*:

fat	fatter	fattest
busy	busier	busiest
little	littler	littlest (size)

Note spellings!

Explanation: There are regular forms for words of two syllables and more.

famous	more famous	most famous
beautiful	more beautiful	most beautiful

Instruction: Think of ten different adjectives and add their comparative and superlative forms.

(a) _____ _____ _____

(b) _____ _____ _____

(c) _____ _____ _____

(d) _____ _____ _____

(e) _____ _____ _____

(f) _____ _____ _____

(g) _____ _____ _____

(h) _____ _____ _____

(i) _____ _____ _____

(j) _____ _____ _____

FOCUS: Time expressions with *it takes, it took* (past), and *it will take* (future)

Explanation: *It takes* is used with a length of time needed to do something. It may be followed by the time expression and an infintive.

Example: It takes many years to learn English.
It took two hours to write the letter.
It will take 20 minutes to mix this.

Instruction: 1. Answer the following questions using the present tense, and then ask other students

   (a)   How long does it take you to come to school?

         It takes _____

   (b)   How long does it take you to fly to Los Angeles?

         It _____

   (c)   How long does it take to get a visa for Canada?

         _____

2.   Make up more questions with *how long*. Work in pairs. One student asks the questions and the other student answers them.

   (a)   1: _____ ?

         2: _____

   (b)   1: _____ ?

         2: _____

   (c)   1: _____ ?

3.   Answer the following questions using the past tense, and then ask other students.

   (a)   1:   How long did it take you to get here from your country?

         2: _____

   (b)   1:   How long did it take you to find an apartment?

         2: _____

   (c)   1:   How long did it take you to eat breakfast today?

         2: _____

4.   Answer the following questions using the future tense, and then ask other students.

   (a)   1:   How long will it take you to learn English?

         2: _____

   (b)   1:   How long will it take you to get home after this lesson?

         2: _____

   (c)   1:   How long will it take to finish this lesson?

         2: _____

What do you hear?

1. The teacher will read the passage *The Corner Store.* Listen carefully and then answer these comprehension questions.

   (a) What was wrong with the person's car?

   _____

   (b) Why didn't the person buy a smaller bottle of cooking oil?

   _____

   (c) What fruit did the person buy? Why?

   _____

   (d) What information did the storekeeper give about pounds and ounces?

   _____

   (e) Why did it take longer for the person to walk home?

   _____

   (f) Do you think the person was a man or woman? Why?

   _____

2. The teacher will read the passage *The Corner Store* again. Listen carefully and write down the word(s) which follow(s) each of these:

   (a) and _____   (g) looked _____

   (b) walk _____   (h) two _____

   (c) carton _____   (i) kilos and _____

   (d) one-liter _____   (j) pounds and _____

   (e) fruit _____   (k) It _____

   (f) cherries were _____

Put it to work

1. Study the vocabulary in the ads on page 125.

2. Look at the same ads. Tell which items are cheaper, more expensive, bigger, more useful, etc., than others; e.g., The aspirin is cheaper than the _____ .

3. Make up some sentences to convince someone to buy one of the products; e.g., This shampoo is very good. It makes your hair soft and it's very cheap.

US GRADE AA
Finest cut, Trimmed

Lamb chops
3.10/lb

QUALITY CORN OIL
NO Saturated Fat.
At Friendly Mart

NATURAL PRODUCTS
VITAMIN E

1.09

CORN OIL

100-CAPSULE BOTTLE
Regularly 6.29
Now only

4.99

EYE DROPS

2.19

Soothe tired eyes.
100% Sterile.
Doesn't stain.

Disposable DIAPERS

2.19

FIZZA COLA

FIZZA COLA
6-pack, 12 oz.

1.01

59¢/lb

FAT, JUICY, DELICIOUS
Tree Ripened Cherries
Only

NOW, ONE LAYER BETTER
Newborn, Daytime,
or Toddler
Your Choice

FAST PAIN RELIEF
ASPIRIN

1.09

Coupon

2 FOR 1.00 RAZOR BLADES

CUT OUT AND... SAVE!

The best pain-killer is here!
Bottle of 100 tablets.

Part 2

Conversation

  1: Hello, what can I do for you?

  2: I have a long list of things I'd like to buy: a bottle of aspirin, a roll of adhesive tape, a toothbrush. . . .

  1: OK, what kind of toothbrush do you want?

  2: A soft brush. What brand do you recommend?

  1: Well, I like both of these.

  2: I'll take the cheaper one.

Vocabulary and Idiom Notes

What can I do for you? = greeting used by sales clerks offering help (also: "May I help you?")

List = paper with names of things to buy or remember or refer to

Aspirin = medicine for pain or headaches

Adhesive tape = white tape for medical use

Structures and functions

FOCUS: Asking for information about products

Explanation: When you are going to do the shopping for someone, and you have a list of things to get, the clerk may need some more information.

Example: A bottle of aspirin

         1: What brand do you want?

         2: The largest size.

  or: 1: What brand do you want?

         2: Osiris, please.

Instruction: Work in pairs. One student is the clerk and makes up some questions about the following items. The other student makes up the customer's answers.

(a) Soap

1: _____

2: _____

(b) Toothbrush

1: _____

2: _____

(c) A ball-point pen

1: _____

2: _____

(d) A box of tissues

1: _____

2: _____

(e) A package of envelopes

1: _____

2: _____

(f) Some "Superbe" shampoo

1: _____

2: _____

FOCUS: Describing drug items. We often refer to an item by its container and its contents, for example: a *bottle of aspirin*. Figure out which containers could go with each product, and make sentences beginning with "I'll take . . ."

Example: "I'll take a bottle of aspirin."

cigarettes	toothpaste	bottle	can
hand cream	cotton balls	jar	carton
alcohol	vaseline	tube	roll
toilet paper	aspirin	box	
soap	adhesive tape	bag	
baby food		package	

(a) _____

(b) _____

(c) _____

(d) _____

(e) _____

(f) _____

(g) _____

(h) _____

(i) _____

(j) _____

(k) _____

What do you say?

Here are some different ways of asking for something in a store. Read them through and decide which of them is

(a) rude
(b) chatty/friendly
(c) polite
(d) threatening

What makes each way different?

1.   Excuse me; I'd like a large bottle of aspirin, please.

2.   Hi, how are you today? Thank goodness it's Friday. I need one large bottle of aspirin, please. I have a terrible headache.

3.   Give me a large bottle of aspirin; I'm in a hurry.

4.   I'm not going to ask you again. I want a large bottle of aspirin. Now.

128

What do you hear?

1. The teacher will read the passage *The Corner Store*. Mark the form of the verb you heard:

   (a) have   has   had
   (b) took   takes   tooked
   (c) brought   bought   buyed
   (d) looked   look   looks
   (e) asks   ask   asked
   (f) give   giving   gave

2. Summarize the passage in two or three sentences of your own.

   _____

   _____

   _____

Put it to work

Go to a drugstore and look around. Write down the names of at least three different sections in the space provided below. Then write down the names of five products from each section in the space provided.

Section 1	Section 2	Section 3
	Products	
_____	_____	_____
_____	_____	_____
_____	_____	_____
_____	_____	_____
_____	_____	_____

Part 3

Conversation

1: Excuse me. Why is this beef cheaper than that?
2: Because it's on special today at $3.20 a pound. It's very good.
1: What else do you suggest?
2: The whole chickens are reduced to 65 cents a pound.
1: O.K. I'll take two of those and freeze them.

Vocabulary and Idiom Notes

On special = reduced = at a lower price than usual
Whole = complete, not cut into pieces
Freeze = put into the freezer to keep for a long time

Pronunciation

Notice the different intonation of *yes/no* questions and questions which begin with a *wh-* word.

Examples: Do you have any chicken?

What else do you have?

Read these questions, paying attention to the intonations. Draw lines to show whether the intonation rises or falls.

(a)   Why is this cheaper?
(b)   What can I do for you?
(c)   Do you want a toothbrush?
(d)   How long will it take?
(e)   Can you fill it now?

Find some more questions in previous lessons and read them to the teacher.

130

Structures and functions

Explanation: When you want to know more information about something, or you want to know the reason for something, you can ask a question with *why*. The answer often begins with *because*.

Example: John comes home at 10 p.m.
1:   Why are you so late?
2:   Because I had to do a lot of extra work.

Instruction: One student asks for more information about each of these statements, and the other student answers with "because . . ."

(a)   Elizabeth is walking to the store.

1:   Why _____

2:   _____

(b)   Jimmy is limping.

1:   _____

2:   _____

(c)   Liz is looking for another apartment.

1:   _____

2:   _____

(d)   Pat is going to the doctor.

1:   _____

2:   _____

(e)   Roy was fired from his new job.

1:   _____

2:   _____

FOCUS: Questions with *what else*

Explanation: *What else* is used to ask for more information, as in these examples:

Examples: 1: I'd like a bottle of aspirin, please.
             2: What else would you like?
             1: Nothing, thank you.
    or: 1: The steak is on sale today.
             2: What else is on sale?
             1: The frozen chicken.

Instruction: One student asks for more information using *what else,* and another student gives the requested information.

(a) 1: I got a color TV for Christmas.

      2: _____

      1: _____

(b) 1: I'm taking an English class this summer.

      2: _____

      1: _____

(c) 1: I saw the Empire State Building in New York City.

      2: _____

      1: _____

(d) 1: I had soup for lunch.

      2: _____

      1: _____

(e) 1: I bought some steak for dinner.

      2: _____

      1: _____

FOCUS: Food prices

Explanation: When we talk about the price of food, we often give the price in terms of the weight.

Example: 1: How much are the apples?
           2: They're 79 cents a pound.

Instruction: Work in pairs. One student asks the price of an item; the other student answers, giving the price per pound.

(a) 1: _____?

      2: _____

(b) 1: _____ ?

    2: _____

(c) 1: _____ ?

    2: _____

(d) 1: _____ ?

    2: _____

(e) 1: _____ ?

    2: _____

What do you hear?

Some items are priced by weight, others by container or volume. The teacher will read some unit prices to you. Write them down like this:

Examples: 79 ¢ a pound
              73 ¢ a bottle
              $1.50 a liter

(a) New York cut steak is _____

(b) Burgundy is _____

(c) Black pepper is _____

(d) Cooking oil is _____

(e) Cornflakes are _____

(f) Peanut butter is _____

(g) Potatoes are _____

(h) Curry powder is _____

(i) Milk is _____

(j) Orange juice is _____

Put it to work

1. Imagine you are going to cook a special dessert for friends. Make up a short shopping list.

(a) _____

(b) _____

(c) _____

(d) _____

(e) _____

(f) _____

(g) _____

(h) _____

2. Go into the grocery store and compare prices on three different brands of soap, and three different brands of frozen orange juice. Compute the differences in unit price.

Example: Sunny soap — 39 cents for 4 oz = 9.7 cents per oz
           Hawaii Soap — 49 cents for 8 oz = 6.1 cents per oz

Report your findings to the class.

(a) Soap. _____

_____

_____

(b) Frozen orange juice. _____

_____

_____

Part 4

Conversation

1: That will be $35.21 altogether.

2: Oh, dear. I don't have enough money. I guess I bought too many things.

1: Do you want to put something back?

3: (A friend): Wait a minute. I can lend you some money.

2: Oh, thanks. Don't forget that I borrowed $10 last night.

3: Don't worry. I'm writing it down. You owe me $25 now.

Vocabulary and Idiom Notes

To lend money = to give someone money which s/he will pay back later

To borrow money = to take money from someone which you plan to pay back later

Don't worry = It's okay.

To owe money = you have borrowed money and not paid it back yet. (This is also called a debt or *being in debt*.) It is also used if you have bought something or someone has done a service. You can say, "How much do I owe you?"

Structures and functions

FOCUS: *Enough* + noun—*too much/too many* + noun

Explanation: *Enough* with a noun indicates sufficient.

Examples: I have enough money = The money is sufficient.

I have all the money I need.

I don't have enough money = I need more money.

I have too little money.

Explanation: *Too much/too many* indicates more than you need.

Examples: You gave me too much money = I don't need all this, take some back.

There are too many students in this class = It is crowded; we don't have enough chairs; some students should leave!

Explanation: *Much* is used for things you can't count like milk, rice, water, money. *Many* is used for things you can count, like people, pencils, apples, dollars. We can say five dollars, but not five monies.

Instruction: Comment on the following sentences using *too much, too many,* or *enough,* as in:

The price is $35.21. You gave me $30.
You didn't give me enough money.

(a)   The elevator takes ten people. There are 12 people in it.

_____

(b)   Mimi earns $900 a month. Her food, rent, and other expenses are $830.

_____

(c)   The bill at the drugstore is $18.20. She has $14.00.

_____

(d)   Mr. Kay's car needs a quart of oil. The mechanic put in two quarts.

_____

(e)   It takes Dr. Verlenden 35 minutes to drive to the hospital. He has a meeting in 15 minutes.

_____

FOCUS: Use of *lend, borrow, owe*

Explanation: See the definitions in the Vocabulary and Idiom Notes.

Examples: 1:   I need some groceries, but I don't have any money.
            2:   You can borrow $25.

or: 1:   Will you pay for my food?
      2:   Okay. Now you owe me $12.

136

Instruction: Fill in the blanks with either a request to borrow money or an offer to lend it.

(a) 1: I don't have enough money to pay the rent.

 2: I can _____

(b) 1: Can you lend me another $20?

 2: _____

(c) 1: I don't have any money for the bus fare.

 2: _____

(d) 1: My sister always borrows money.

 2: I know. Yesterday I had to _____

(e) Taxi driver: This is the address.

 You: _____

What do you say?

Think of some different ways to ask somebody to lend you ten dollars. Be:

(a) polite   (c) rude
(b) friendly   (d) threatening

What do you hear?

1. The teacher will read some prices, weights, and measures. Write down the order in which you hear them, putting 1, 2, etc., next to each one. Listen carefully.

97¢	1 kg	48¢	30 cc
24 oz	2.5 lb	48 oz	10 lb
$1.99	10 g	2 liters	28 oz
2 lb	1 lb 4 oz	22 lb	$1.19

2. The teacher will read some more prices, some weights, and some measures. Write down the numbers and the correct abbreviations.

Examples: $1.63   24 oz   1.5 liters

_____ _____ _____ _____ _____

_____ _____ _____ _____ _____

137

Put it to work

1. Discussion. Who does the shopping in your household? Why? When? How often? Which stores do you use? How is shopping different in the United States from your country?

2. Write a short account of the last time you went shopping. Tell what you bought and how much you spent.

_____

_____

_____

_____

_____

TOPIC 9

Visiting Friends

Part 1

Conversation

1: Oh, Mimi, I'm glad I bumped into you. Can you guys come over for dinner on Friday?

2: Let me see. Friday, that's the 8th, isn't it? Oh, dear, I'd like to, but we're going to the ball game.

1: Oh, too bad! How about the week after!

2: That sounds great. What can we bring?

1: Nothing. We'll make something simple.

Pronunciation

Intonation of tag questions: Remember, when you are almost sure that you are right, use falling intonation.

Example: That's the eighth, isn't it?

When you are not sure and are really asking for information, use rising intonation.

Example: He doesn't live here, does he?

Practice these tag questions. Draw lines to show the intonation.

(Almost sure)   1:   The bank is open today, isn't it?

(Almost sure)   2:   You had an operation, didn't you?

(Not sure)   3:   He isn't looking for an apartment, is he?

(Almost sure)   4:   This one is better, isn't it?

(Not sure)   5:   We shouldn't sit here, should we?

Vocabulary and Idiom Notes

To bump into = to meet by accident

You guys = you and your family (or friends)—very informal

The week after = one week later (here, the next Friday)

That sounds great = that's very good

Structures and functions

FOCUS: Inviting and accepting

Explanation: There are several ways of inviting people to dinner or to a party. They are grouped from level A = formal to level C = informal. The level of the conversation is informal (level C).

Examples:
- A   I was wondering if you and your wife could come to dinner on Friday.
- A/B   We're having a few people over on Friday night. Would you be able to join us?
- B   Could you come over for dinner Friday night?
- B   Would you like to (be able to) come to dinner on Friday?
- C   Hey, you wanna get together on Friday?

Explanation: There are also several ways to accept the invitation. For an informal party, the guests usually offer to bring something. The host(ess) may or may not agree.

Examples:
- A   Thank you. That would be very nice.
- A   Thank you. We'd love to.
- B   We'd love to. Can we bring something?
- C   Sounds great. What shall we bring?

Instruction: Make up some formal and informal conversations of invitation and acceptance.

(a)   Employee: _____

     Boss: _____

(b)   Adult student: _____

     Teacher: _____

(c)   New friend: _____

     New friend: _____

(d)   Very good friend: _____

     Very good friend: _____

Discuss with the teacher which of the student conversations are good and which are not. There may be more than one for each pair. Practice the good ones with another student.

FOCUS: Refusing

Explanation: If you can't go, it is polite to say that you want to go and to explain why you can't. Sound sorry. It is impolite to say only "I can't."

Examples: A   Oh, that sounds delightful, but unfortunately my husband has a business engagement.

A/B   Oh, I'd love to, but I have other plans that night.

A/B/C Oh, I'd love to, but I have to work.

B/C   Oh, I can't that night. Maybe some other time.

Explanation: Notice the use of *but* to show the contrast between what you would like to do and the reason why you can't do it.

Instruction: Make up some conversations between the same pairs of people as above. This time the second person refuses.

(a) Employee: _____

Boss: _____

(b) Adult student: _____

Teacher: _____

(c) New friend: _____

New friend: _____

(d) Very good friend: _____

Very good friend: _____

FOCUS: *But* in other kinds of explanations

Explanation: *But* can be used to explain why something didn't or won't happen.

Example: I would like to get a new apartment, but I don't have time to look for one.

Instruction: Finish these sentences with an explanation.

(a) I would like to buy a new car, but _____

(b) My aunt wants to go to Taiwan, but _____

(c) My mother wanted to invite you, but _____

(d) He would like to open a savings account, but _____

(e) I wanted to buy that dress, but _____

What do you hear?

1. The teacher will read the passage *An Invitation* twice. Answer the following questions:

(a) When is July 6th? (i.e., what day) _____

_____

(b) What is the speaker going to do on July 4th? _____

_____

(c) Where did the speaker spend last Thanksgiving Day? _____

_____

(d) Why did the speaker refuse Chuck and Lily's Christmas invitation?

_____

_____

(e) Why will the speaker have to rent a tuxedo? _____

_____

(f) Is the speaker male or female? How do you know? _____

_____

2. As the teacher reads the passage again, write the words which come after the following:

(a) invited me _____ (two words)

(b) I'll go _____

(c) Janice _____

(d) Thanksgiving _____

(e) asked me _____

(f) I went _____

(g) invited me _____

(h) dinner _____

(i) borrow one _____

Put it to work

1. Study the written invitations which follow.

2. Discuss how the ceremonies associated with them differ in other countries.

143

Come for Cocktails!

DATE: _____

TIME: _____

PLACE: _____

REGRETS ONLY

A SHOWER

on _____

at _____

by _____

for _____

RSVP

Mr. and Mrs. Timothy Smith
request the honor of your presence
at the marriage of their daughter

JOAN MARIE

to

ANTHONY KIRKLAND

On Saturday the Twentieth of July
at 3:00 p.m.
Wayside Methodist Church

Reception follows at the Elks Lodge
2100 Maple Boulevard

RSVP: 585 High Street, Aliceville

Part 2

Conversation

1: Hi. Come on in.

2: Are we early?

1: No. A few people have arrived already. They're in the living room. What can I get you to drink?

2: Well, what are you serving?

1: Wine, beer, Seven-up, orange juice.

2: I'd like a glass of wine, please.

3: I'm afraid I drank too much last night, so I'd better have Seven-up.

Vocabulary and Idiom Notes

Come on in, come in = said at the door when
people arrive

I/he/she drank too much = refers to liquor when we
don't name the liquid

Structures and functions

FOCUS: Use of *so*

Explanation: You know how to give a reason using *because*:

> I'd better eat less *because I'm getting too fat.*

You can use *so* when you give the reasons first and then the conclusion:

> I'm getting too fat, *so I'd better eat less.*

(Note: Use a comma before *so,* but not with *because.*)

Instruction: 1. Complete the sentences below, filling in a conclusion with *so.*

(a) He didn't have enough money, so _____

(b) She doesn't like beer, so _____

(c) I couldn't find my keys, so _____

(d) My mother had an operation last week, so _____

(e) I was late for class, so _____

2. Change the sentences you wrote, using *because.*

(a) _____

(b) _____

(c) _____

(d) _____

(e) _____

FOCUS: Indefinite numbers: *a few, a lot of, a couple of*

Explanation:
> A few = a small number
> A little = a small amount (for noncountable things)
> A lot of = a large number of (for countable things) or a large amount of (for uncountable things)

Note: The use of these expressions depends on the situation. If there are ten people in a large room, you could say a *few,* but if there are ten people in the bathroom, you might say:

Example: There are *a lot of* people in the bathroom.

Instruction: Describe the situations below using *a couple, a few, a little, a lot of*

Example: Two apples in the basket.
> There are a couple of apples in the basket.

(a) Three or four people on the beach

_____

146

(b)   Twenty people in the doctor's office

_____

(c)   Ten chairs around the table.

_____

(d)   Two or three cars in the parking lot

_____

(e)   Some flour in the bottom of the bag

_____

What do you hear?   The teacher will read some sentences which include names and dates of American holidays (Appendix 1). Write the sentences.

(a)   _____

(b)   _____

(c)   _____

(d)   _____

(e)   _____

(f)   _____

(g)   _____

(h)   _____

Put it to work   Answer the invitations you studied in Part 1; then:

(a)   Make up a telephone conversation, accepting or refusing an informal invitation (e.g., to a birthday party).

1:   _____

2:   _____

1:   _____

2:   _____

(b)   Imagine you received the wedding invitation on page 144. Write an answer to it on a separate sheet of paper.

Part 3

Conversation

1: Would you like some more turkey?

2: Just a little, thanks. I've already eaten too much.

1: How about some Jello?

2: Oh, no, thank you. I haven't gotten used to Jello yet.

1: I know what you mean. It's hard to get used to foreign food. I had trouble with the raw fish in Japan.

Pronunciation

The different pronunciations of *ou* and *oo*.

although	should	group
	could	soup
	would	tooth
	look	
sound	ought	enough
found	fought	tough
cow	often	

Recall or make up sentences using each word above.

Vocabulary and Idiom Notes

Turkey = (meat of) a large American bird usually served at Thanksgiving and Christmas holidays

Jello = a salad or dessert made from fruit juice and gelatin; it has a rubbery feeling

Raw = not cooked

Foreign = from another country

To get used to = to start to like something you didn't like before

Note: This phrase looks like *used to,* used for past repeated action ("I used to swim there"); however, its meaning is very different.

To have trouble with = to have a problem = it is difficult

Structures and functions

Explanation: See Vocabulary and Idiom Notes.

Instruction: 1. Tell what things are hard to get used to in America.

Example: It's hard to get used to the big cars.

(a)   It's hard to get used to _____

(b)   _____

(c)   _____

2.   Tell what it's hard for foreigners to get used to in your country.

(a)   _____

(b)   _____

3.   Now use the *present perfect* to tell what you haven't gotten used to yet. Either change sentences a, b, and c above, or make up new ones.

Example: I haven't gotten used to the big cars yet.

(a)   _____

(b)   _____

(c)   _____

4.   Think of some things you didn't like at first, but you have gotten used to.

(a)   At first I didn't like _____ , but I have gotten used to it/them.

(b)   _____

(c)   _____

5.   Tell what you will never get used to in America.

Example: I'll never get used to the rock music.

(a)   _____

(b)   _____

(c)   _____

FOCUS: Accepting and refusing food

Explanation: When someone offers you some more food, he or she usually begins by saying: "Would you like . . ." If you want some more, you can say:

Examples: Yes, please.
Yes, thank you.
Yes, please, it's delicious.
Yes, please, just a little. I've already eaten so much!

Explanation: If you don't want any more, you can say:

Examples: Oh, no thank you. It was so good, but I'm full.
Oh, I wish I could, but I've already eaten too much.

Note: The host(ess) will probably offer only once; so if you really do want some more, accept the first offer.

Instruction: 1. Work in pairs. Make up some conversations. In the first three, one student offers some (more) food, and another student accepts.

Example: 1: Would you like some more rice?
2: Yes, please, it's delicious.

(a) 1: _____

2: _____

(b) 1: _____

2: _____

(c) 1: _____

2: _____

2. In the last two conversations, one student offers some (more) food, and another student refuses.

Example: 1: Would you like some Jello?
2: Oh, I can't. Dinner was so good, but I'm full.

(a) 1: _____

2: _____

(b) 1: _____

2: _____

Go over your conversations with the teacher to see if they are correct. Then practice them.

What do you hear?

1. The teacher will read a recipe which includes the following ingredients. Number them in the order you hear them.

    _____ water   _____ rice   _____ celery

    _____ tomatoes   _____ onion   _____ paprika

    _____ chicken   _____ bay leaf   _____ bread crumbs

    _____ cheese   _____ sugar   _____ butter

2. Here are some short (abbreviated) forms for food measurements.

    cup = c.
    tablespoon = T. or tbsp.
    teaspoon = t. or tsp.

    Now the teacher will read the recipe again. Put in the correct amount for each one of the ingredients.

    _____ rice   _____ tomatoes   _____ sugar

    _____ water   _____ bay leaf   _____ chicken

    _____ onion   _____ salt   _____ cheese

    _____ butter   _____ paprika   _____ bread crumbs

Put it to work

1. Study the recipe which follows.

2. Discuss the different customs for giving parties in other countries; for example, what kinds of food are served? Do guests bring food or drink?

3. Discuss the customs concerning the time one should arrive in your country. Should you arrive on time, a little late, or does it not matter?

    Rice Pilaf

    Boil 3/4 cup rice with 1 1/2 cups water. Sauté 3 tablespoons chopped onion in 1 tablespoon butter. Add to the rice.
    Simmer 2 1/2 cups tomatoes, 1/2 bay leaf, 3 stalks of celery, 1/3 teaspoon salt, 1/4 teaspoon paprika, 1/2 teaspoon brown sugar. Strain.
    Add 1 cup cooked shrimp or boiled chicken livers. Place in a baking dish.
    Sprinkle with 1/3 cup grated cheese and bread crumbs. Broil to brown.

Part 4

Conversation

Guest: Well, it's getting late. We'd better be going.
Host: Yeah, I guess we all have to get up early.
Guest: Thanks a lot. It was a great party. It was nice to meet you, Joan.
Hostess: Nice meeting you.
Host: Let's get together again soon. We haven't seen you much recently.
Guest: I know. We've been busy lately. But we'll call you soon. Bye.
Hostess: Good-bye.

Vocabulary and Idiom Notes

Host = person who invites other to his home
Hostess = same as host, but female
It's getting late = an expression meaning that you plan to leave
It was { nice meeting you
        { nice to meet you = say this *when you leave* after meeting someone for the first time. If you met the person before and you have just spoken to him/her again, say, "It was nice meeting you again." (You can also say "Nice to meet you" when you are introduced. You *can't* say "Nice meeting you" until later.)
Recently, lately = in the near past

Structures and functions

FOCUS: Use of *recently, lately*

Explanation: Both these words mean "in the near past" and indicate duration. They are used with the present perfect, often in the negative. They usually go at the end of the sentence.

Instruction: Use *recently* or *lately* to tell what you haven't been doing.

> Examples: See movies: I haven't seen any movies lately.

Write sentences that are true for you.

(a)   Clean the apartment

_____

(b)   Go swimming

_____

(c)   Ride a bicycle

_____

(d)   Be at home

_____

(e)   (Make up a true sentence)

_____

FOCUS: Thanking and leaving

Explanation: There are usually four things involved in leaving after a party or dinner:

(a)   You say you are leaving and often make an excuse.

Example: It's getting late.

Explanation:

(b)   You say thank you, and mention that you had a good time.

Examples: It was a delicious dinner.
It was really a nice party.
I had a really good time.

Explanation:

(c)   The host(ess) will say, or you can say, something about another visit.

Examples: Let's get together again soon.
I hope we'll see you soon.
Let's do this again.
We'd like to have you over to our place next time.

Explanation:

(d) You all say good-bye or good night.

Instruction: Write two leaving conversations. Use phrases from above.

(a) Guest: 1: _____

           2: _____

     Host: 1: _____

           2: _____

     Guest: 1: _____

     Host: 2: _____

(b) Guest: 1: _____

           2: _____

     Host: 1: _____

     Guest: 1: _____

     Host: 2: _____

What
do you hear?

1. The teacher will read another recipe (Appendix 1). Write down the ingredients and amounts as she reads.

    Example: 1 c. water

    _____ _____ _____ _____

    _____ _____ _____ _____

2. The teacher will read the recipe again. List the things you have to do to the ingredients.

    Example: Mix, cut

    _____ _____ _____ _____

    _____ _____ _____ _____

Put it to work

1. Write a recipe for something you could serve at a dinner party. You might be able to use things from your shopping list in Topic 8.

2. Discuss setting the table for dinner. Did you use the same things in your native country as Americans use in theirs?

3. Write a thank-you note for a dinner party.

Example:

June 20

Dear Mary and Bill,

Thanks so much for having us over on Friday. We are still talking about the wonderful pictures of your trip. I'll call you soon to get the recipe for the great stew. We're going to make it for Stan's parents.

Warmly,
Jill

Quiz, Topics 7 to 9

A. Which one is good English?

1. a. I should have eaten my lunch.   (Topic 7, Part 1)
   b. I should eaten my lunch.
   c. I should have ate my lunch.

2. Boss: Good morning, Mr. Wong. How are you?   (Topic 7, Part 1)
   Employee: a. Okay. What's happening?
              b. Hi. How about you?
              c. Fine, thank you. How are you?

3. 1:   Which one stole the money?   (Topic 7, Part 3)
   2:    a. The man in the blue eyes.
          b. The man with the blue eyes.
          c. The man of the blue eyes.

4. a. It takes 10 minutes to walk to school.   (Topic 8, Part 1)
   b. It was took 10 minutes to walk to school.
   c. It is take 10 minutes to walk to school.

5. a. I take one bottle of aspirin.   (Topic 8, Part 2)
   b. I'm take one bottle of aspirin.
   c. I'll take one bottle of aspirin.

6. The bill is $24.95. You paid $25.00.   (Topic 8, Part 4)
   a. You paid too much money.
   b. You didn't pay enough money.
   c. You paid too many monies.

7. 1:   Can you come to the party?   (Topic 9, Part 1)
   2:    a. I'd like to, and I am busy.
          b. I'd like to, but I'll be at work.
          c. I'd like to, but I can do it.

8. I'm very tired, so   (Topic 9, Part 2)
   a. I'll drink a lot.
   b. I'll go to a party.
   c. I'll take a rest.

9. a. A lot of people went to the beach.   (Topic 9, Part 2)
   b. Lot of people went to the beach.
   c. A lots of people went to the beach.

10. a. Would you like some coffee?   (Topic 9, Part 3)
    b. Do you like some coffee?
    c. Will you like some coffee?

B. Finish the conversations:

11. 1: _____

    2: Oh, I've been busy at home.   (Topic 7, Part 1)

12. 1: Pardon me?

    2: _____ (Topic 7, Part 2)

13. 1: What did he look like?

    2: _____ with a _____ (Topic 7, Part 3)

14. 1: This _____

    2: _____ Nice to meet you. (Topic 7, Part 4)

15. 1: _____ ?

    2: About three hours. (Topic 8, Part 1)

16. 1: _____

    2: Here you are. That's 59 ¢. (Topic 8, Part 2)

17. 1: Oh dear, I don't have enough money.

    2: Never mind, _____ (Topic 8, Part 4)

18. 1: _____ ?

    2: Oh, I'd love to, but I have a class. (Topic 9, Part 1)

19. 1: Would you like some of my special bat's eye soup?

    2: Oh, _____ (Topic 9, Part 3)

20. 1: Let's get together soon.

    2: _____ (Topic 9, Part 4)

TOPIC 10

Travel

Part 1

Conversation

1: Excuse me. Could you tell me when the plane from Chicago arrives?

2: Sure. Let me see. It should have arrived at 10:20, but it was delayed by fog. The new estimated time of arrival is 10:55, at Gate C.

1: Do you know where Gate C is?

2: Yes, sir. The first gate on your left.

Vocabulary and Idiom Notes

Delayed = stopped for a time; made to start later

Fog = low, wet clouds at the ground level

To estimate = to guess or figure out

Yes, sir = a polite way of saying *yes* to a man (say, *Yes, ma'am* to women)

Note: When asking about arriving and leaving, we often use present tense even though it is a question about the future. Example: *When* does *it arrive?*

Structures and functions

FOCUS: Review of *should have* + past participle

Explanation: In Topic 7 you studied *should have* used for giving advice (for example: You should have eaten breakfast). Here it is used to indicate something that was planned but that did not happen.

Instruction: Work in pairs. Comment on the following situations using *should have* and a time, according to the following example:

Example: 1: Why is this plane still on the ground?

         2: I don't know. It *should have left* at 10:00. (But it didn't.)

(a) 1: Why didn't my mail come today?

    2: I don't know. It _____

159

(b) 1: Why is Ivan still here?

2: I don't know. He _____

(c) 1: Why is the interview still going on?

2: _____

(d) 1: Why isn't the bank open? It's 10:15.

2: _____

(e) 1: Why hasn't the bus come yet?

2: _____

FOCUS: Combining polite questions with information questions.

Explanation: Notice the change in word order of the questions in these examples:

1. Could you tell me + Where is Gate C?
    Could you tell me where Gate C is?
2. Do you know . . . + When does it arrive?
    Do you know when it arrives?

Instruction: 1. Make the following into single polite information questions:

(a) Do you know / When does the bus leave?

_____

(b) Do you know / Where are the tickets?

_____

(c) Do you know / Why was the plane delayed?

_____

(d) Can you tell me / Why does the engine make that noise?

_____

(e) Can you tell me / Where did the doctor go?

_____

2. Work in pairs. One student asks some questions about the school or the city. Another student gives a true answer.

(a) 1: Can you tell me when _____ ?

2: _____

(b) 1: Do you know where _____ ?

2: _____

160

(c) 1: Could you tell me why _____?

2: _____

(d) 1: Can you tell us why _____?

2: _____

(e) 1: Excuse me _____?

2: _____

What do you hear?

1. The teacher will read the conversation *Buying an Airplane Ticket* twice. Quickly make notes on the dates, times, and flight numbers to help you remember them. Then answer the questions.

(a) Notes

_____ _____ _____ _____

_____ _____ _____ _____

(b) Questions

1. How many people want to travel to Miami?
2. What day are they leaving?
3. When does the day flight leave?
4. When does it arrive in New York?
5. What is the flight number of the day flight?
6. When does it arrive in Miami?
7. Which flight did the customer choose?

Put it to work

1. Study the additional airport vocabulary which follows. Make up sentences using the words.

Airport Vocabulary

Nouns	Verbs	Airlines
arrival	to arrive	**International**
departure	to depart	American, TWA, Pan Am, _____
boarding lounge	to board	
boarding pass	to land	**West**
duty-free shop	to take off	Western, Air California, PSA, _____
stopover	to line up	
flight	to change planes	**South**
airline	to deplane	Delta, _____
airfare		
destination		**East**
		Eastern, U.S. Air, _____

161

Arrivals					Departures			
Flight	Orig	ETA	Gate		Flight	Dest	ETD	Gate
172	Chicago	11:10	22		110	Portland	11:02	3
95	Seattle	11:15	16		102	New York	11:25	17
221	Honolulu	11:22	29		307	Mexico City	11:30	19
11	Los Angeles	11:39	28		338	Las Vegas	11:45	23
383	Phoenix	12:20	5		6	Wash, D.C.	12:05	27

2. Study the schedule of arrivals and departures. Practice asking questions about the flights and answering them.

Examples: 1: When does Flight 221 arrive?
2: It arrives at 11:22.
1: Where is Flight 172 coming from?
2: It is coming from Chicago.

(a) 1: _____

2: _____

(b) 1: _____

2: _____

(c) 1: _____

2: _____

Part 2

Conversation

1: Hello. Do you have a three-day Disneyland tour?
2: That's right, for only $109.95. That includes air fare, a room at the Fair Friends Motel, and all admissions.
1: What was the last thing?
2: Admission to the park is included.
1: Sorry. I still don't understand. What does admission mean?
2: Tickets. You get in free.
1: Oh, I see. Thank you.

Vocabulary and Idiom Notes

Disneyland = a famous amusement park in Los Angeles

A three-day tour = a package of things to do in three days all included in one price

To include = to have in it

Air fare = the price of the plane ticket

Motel = a hotel usually outside the city centers for people with cars. You generally park near your room. (Note: *motor* + *hotel* = motel)

Admission = the price of a ticket to enter a place, usually for entertainment (e.g., a park, a zoo, a museum)

Structures and functions

FOCUS: Present tense, passive voice

Explanation: When the object of the sentence is more important than the subject, or when we don't know the subject, we can put the object first. We don't need to use the subject.

Example: (The price) includes admission = Admission is included.

Explanation: If you are talking about a permanent condition or things which happen regularly (the present tense), use *is* or *are* and the past participle for passive voice.

Instruction: 1. Mention some things that are sold in a department store.

(a) Appliances _____

(b) _____

(c) _____

2. Tell some things that are done by machines.

    (a) Streets _____

    (b) _____

    (c) _____

3. Tell some things that are made or grown in your native country.

    (a) Coffee _____

    (b) _____

    (c) _____

FOCUS: Past tense, passive voice sentences

Explanation: If you are talking about things that happened in the past, use *was* or *were* and the past participle.

Example: The plane was delayed by fog.

Instruction: 1. Fill in the blanks with the passive voice of the verbs in parentheses.

Last week I went on vacation. We had a car accident, and my right leg (a) _____ (break). The car (b) _____ (damage) badly. I was in the hospital for two days and (c) _____ (take care of) very well by the doctor. Then I went to my hotel. At the beach my wallet (d) _____ (steal), and I lost $150. I told the police. The next day a man (e) _____ (catch) on the beach stealing money from someone else. He (f) _____ (arrest) by the police, but I didn't get my money back.

2. Now make up some sentences in the past tense of the passive voice.

    (a) Tell what happened at the dentist's office.

        My teeth were _____

    (b) Tell about a car accident.

        His leg _____

        The car _____

    (c) Tell what happened at the hospital.

        _____

(d) Tell what happened during a robbery.

_____

(e) Tell what happened at a gas station.

_____

FOCUS: Getting explanations politely

Explanation: There are several polite ways to ask a speaker to repeat or explain something:

Examples: You can say: "Excuse me?"
                    or: "Pardon me?"

Some people say "What?" or "Huh?" but it is not polite.

If you don't know the meaning of a word, you can say:

"What does _____ mean?"
or: "I don't understand _____ ."

Instruction: Work in pairs. One student asks the meaning of a word, and another student explains.

Example: 1:   What does *airport* mean?
            2:   It means: the place where you go to catch a plane.

(a) Duty-free

1: _____

2: _____

(b) Office

1: _____

2: _____

(c) Invitation

1: _____

2: _____

(d) Operation

1: _____

2: _____

(e) Ambulance

1: _____

2: _____

Explanation: There are other things you can say if you didn't quite hear what someone just said:

Examples:　I didn't hear　　that name.
　　　　　　　　　　　　　the last word.
　　　　　　　　　　　　　the time.
　　　　　　　　　　　　　the number.

　　　　　　　What was　　that?
　　　　　　　　　　　　　the first thing you said?
　　　　　　　　　　　　　the last thing?

Instruction: Finish these conversations. Work in pairs. 1 reads the sentence, 2 doesn't understand, and 1 repeats it. Put in one of the above phrases and the repeated word or explanation.

Example:　1:　Go to 1400 Smith Street.
　　　　　　2:　I didn't hear the number.
　　　　　　1:　1400.

(a)　1:　Mrs. McKlutz can't come.

　　　2:　_____

　　　1:　_____

(b)　1:　You should bring sunglasses and a bathing suit.

　　　2:　_____

　　　1:　_____

(c)　1:　Flight 725 from Chicago arrives at 7:10.

　　　2:　_____

　　　1:　_____

(d)　1:　You can open an account in room 12B.

　　　2:　_____

　　　1:　_____

(e)　1:　I'm having a problem with one of my molars.

　　　2:　_____

　　　1:　_____

166

What do you say?

The following conversations are all on the same topic but vary according to different settings. See if you can tell the correct situation for each conversation. Give reasons for your choice.

(a) 1: How long will you be staying in this country, sir?
    2: Two weeks.

(b) 1: How many nights did you want to stay here?
    2: Until the morning of the 25th.

(c) 1: How long can you stay with us?
    2: Until the 25th, if you can stand it.

(d) 1: What day do you want to leave?
    2: Check if there's a flight on the 25th.

(e) 1: When do you have to go back?
    2: Not until the 25th. We have two whole weeks.

Settings

(1) A hotel desk. Guest has inquired about a room.

(2) Immigration officer checking the passport of an arriving traveller.

(3) Travel agent talking with passenger who is making a booking.

(4) Two lovers who live a long way apart and have just met again.

(5) Person who has arrived to stay with friends.

What do you hear?

The teacher will read *Buying an Airplane Ticket*. Fill in the blanks.

"Good morning" _____ like to make a reservation for _____ Miami.

"When did you want to _____ ?"

"Thursday the _____ ."

"Round-trip or one-way?"

"One-way."

"O.K. You have two _____ . Flight 271 leaves _____ 7:05 a.m., arriving _____ New York at 10:26. You _____ with Flight 56, departing _____ 11:14 and arriving _____ Miami _____ 1:23. The _____ is a night flight leaving at 11:29 p.m. and _____ in Miami at 4:06 the _____ morning. The night _____ is cheaper than the day _____ ."

"O.K., thanks. Please _____ us seats on the night flight."

Put it to work

1. Study a travel brochure. What information does it give you about hotels, food, sports activities, sightseeing? Would you like to go to the places described in it? Why or why not?

2. Imagine you have a certain amount of money (for example, $800) for a vacation. Can you go on one of the trips in your brochure? Which hotel room will you take? How long will you stay?

Part 3

Conversation

1: Excuse me: Have you filled out your customs and immigration forms?

2: Well, I'm trying to, but I don't understand *For official use only.*

1: That means you don't have to write anything there. It will be filled in by the officer.

2: Oh, I see. Will my luggage be searched?

1: I don't know. Sometimes they just search every two or three people.

Pronunciation

Notice that past participles ending in *en* sound like there is only an *n*.

Written   writ'n

Practice these words:

written   forgotten
eaten   beaten

Sentences:

1. I haven't written a letter yet.
2. He has forgotten his lunch.
3. Our team was beaten by the Yankees.

Structures and functions

FOCUS: Use of *every* in time expressions

Explanation: The word *every* used with a number or date or time indicates that something happened regularly or again and again, and tells how far apart each occurrence was.

Examples:	Every	hour	Every other	hour	Every two	hours
		month		month		months
		week		week		weeks
		day		day		days

Explanation: If you go to class on Monday, Wednesday, and Friday, you go *every other day*.

Instruction: 1. Give an expression with *every* to describe each situation.

(a) 1:00   3:00   5:00   7:00

Every _____

(b) January   March   May   July

Every _____

(c) Mr. Smith   Mr. Jones   Mr. Lou   Mr. Bye

Every _____

(d) Twice in a month (the first week and the third week)

_____

(e) Jan 1   Jan 4   Jan 7   Jan 10

_____

169

2. Now tell some things you or your family do regularly but not every day.

(a) _____

(b) _____

(c) _____

(d) _____

(e) _____

FOCUS: Passive voice—future

Explanation: Add *be* and use the past participle.

Instruction: Tell what will happen to these things or people as in the following example:

A child is standing in the middle of the road.
He will be hit by a car.

(a) He started to write the letter an hour ago.

It _____

(b) A wallet is lying on the sidewalk.

It _____

(c) A delicious cake is on the table.

It _____

(d) A boat is on the ocean in a bad storm.

It _____

(e) A man is falling from a tall building.

He _____

What do you hear?

Follow the instructions the teacher will read (from Appendix 1) for each example below.

Example: Circle every other letter.

              A   B   C   D   E

(a) 5   7   10   12   14   22   27

(b) A   B   C   D   E   F   G   H   I   J

(c) .   .   .   +   .   .   .   +   .   .   .   +   .   .   .

(d) □ □ □ □ □ □ □ □ □ □ □ □

(e) △ △ △ △ △ △ △ △ △ △ △ △ △

(f) ——— ——— ——— ——— ———

(g) ——— ——— ——— ——— ———

(h)

(i)　January　February　March　April　May　June

(j)　Monday　Tuesday　Wednesday　Thursday　Friday　Saturday　Sunday

Put it to work

Write a conversation about something that happened on a trip you took, or make up a conversation using one of these titles:

"A Lost Passport"
"Meeting an Interesting Traveler"
"Getting Lost"
"A Beautiful Place"

_____

_____

_____

_____

_____

Part 4

Conversation

1: Do you mind if I smoke?
2: I don't, but it's not allowed. There are No Smoking signs on the seats.
1: I wonder if there's a smoking section in the back. I'm dying for a cigarette.
2: I know what you mean. I just quit smoking a few months ago.

Vocabulary and Idiom Notes

Do you mind if = Is it O.K.? (If it is O.K., answer, *No, not at all; go ahead;* or *I don't mind.*)
I wonder = I don't know; I'm trying to guess.
I'm dying for = I'm very uncomfortable (because I need a cigarette).

Structures and functions

FOCUS: Asking permission

Explanation: *Do you mind + if* is more polite than *Can I.*

Instruction: Work in pairs. One student asks polite questions, another answers, as in the following example:

Close the door
1: Do you mind if I close the door?
2: No. (Go ahead.)

172

Notice that if it is OK, you can answer *No* because "Do you mind" means something like: "Will you be angry or upset?"

(a) Take off my coat

     1: _____

     2: _____

(b) Move my chair

     1: _____

     2: _____

(c) Look at your book

     1: _____

     2: _____

(d) (Make up your own.)

     1: _____

     2: _____

(e) (Make up your own.)

     1: _____

     2: _____

FOCUS: Combining sentences

Explanation: Notice that the requests you practice in Part 1 (Could you tell me . . .)
are used in about the same way as phrases of uncertainty (I wonder, I don't
know). The wh-question word is kept, and the word order is changed. *If* is used
for yes/no questions.

Examples: Each of the phrases on the left can be used with each of the phrases on
the right:

Could you tell me   where it is?
Do you know   who he is?
                           why they did it?

I wonder   if he came in
I don't know   if they are here

Instruction: Comment on the following situations using *I wonder* plus *if* or a question
word, as in the following example:

You knock on a friend's door. There is no answer.
You: I wonder if they are on vacation.
  or: I wonder where they are.

(a) You arrive at school, but no one is there.

     You: I wonder if _____

       or: I wonder why _____

(b) You call a friend on the phone, but the phone rings and rings.

     You: I wonder if _____

       or: I wonder where _____

(c) You have applied for a job.

     You: I wonder who _____

       or: I wonder if _____

(d) The doctor just tested your heart.

     You: I wonder what _____

       or: I wonder if _____

(e) Someone gave you a dirty look.

     You: I wonder why _____

       or: I wonder if _____

**What
do you hear?**

The teacher will read the passage *The Terrible Vacation*. List the bad things that happened. Use passive voice.

_____

_____

_____

_____

_____

Put it to work

1. Visit a travel agent, and pick up brochures from your native country. Tell the class about good places to travel in your native country. Use the brochure for an illustration.

2. Describe a vacation you would like to take.

3. Write a letter describing a wonderful vacation.

TOPIC 11

Clothing

Part 1

Conversation

1: I'd like to try on those beige suede gloves, please.

2: What size do you wear?

1: I'm not sure. Maybe medium. (Tries on gloves.) No, these don't fit. I guess I need bigger ones.

2: I'm sorry. We're out of the large size in beige. Here is another nice style, in navy blue.

1: No, thanks. I think I'll keep looking.

Vocabulary and Idiom Notes

Clothing colors: beige = very light brown
  navy blue = very dark blue

Suede = a soft, rough leather

To try on = to put on for a minute to check the size or looks

To wear = to have on the body (I am wearing a new dress.) (I always wear size 10.)

To fit = to be the right size

Style = a certain design or kind of clothes

(We are) out of = (we) had some, but they have all been sold

Note: in + color
  size = used (especially by salespeople) to describe the color or size of something

Structures and functions

FOCUS: Verbs used with clothing

Explanation: See the meanings of the words in the vocabulary notes.

Instruction: 1. Fill in the correct positive or negative form of one of the three verbs: *fit, wear, try on,* as in the following examples:

I always wear a coat in the winter.
This dress doesn't fit very well.

    (a)   I go into that store often. I like to _____ the shoes.

    (b)   Oh, too bad. The beige dress _____ .

    (c)   All the high school girls _____ high-heeled shoes to school.

    (d)   You're lucky. That size 9 _____ you.

    (e)   Please, don't _____ any more gloves. I want to go home.

    2.   Use the habitual present tense with other verbs, as in the following example:

Tell the class your shoe size.
I wear size nine shoes.

    (a)   Tell the class how often you go to the dentist.

    _____

    (b)   Tell the class how you travel to school.

    _____

    (c)   Tell the class when you eat dinner.

    _____

    (d)   Tell the class what your family does on the weekend.

    _____

    (e)   Tell the class what you do at the bank.

    _____

FOCUS: *Another (one), the other (one), the others*

Explanation: When there is a large or unknown number of things, you can use *another* to refer to the second one of them.

Example: He ate one cookie (from a plate of cookies), and then he took another one.

Explanation: *The other* refers to the second of two or the last one of a group.

Example: You take the red books. I'll carry the others (the blues, the greens, etc.).

Instruction: Answer these questions using one of the three forms—*another (one), the other (one), the others.*

(a) 1: Does Dave go to the state college?

    2: No, _____

(b) 1: Which of the two cars do you like, this one?

    2: No, _____

(c) 1: Did you take the green ones?

    2: No, _____

(d) 1: Is there anything wrong with your steak, sir?

    2: Yes, _____

(e) 1: Is Mimi the only foreign student in your class?

    2: No, _____

What do you hear?

1. The teacher will read the passage *Buying a Suit* twice. Answer the questions.

    (a) Why did the speaker want a new suit?

    _____

    (b) Were there any special offers?

    _____

    (c) What was wrong with the second suit he tried on?

    _____

    (e) Which suit did he buy?

    _____

2. Listen again and write down the words that precede or follow these:

    (a) finally _____

    (b) to _____

    (c) to buy _____

    (d) _____ sale

    (e) like _____

(f) _____ line

(g) _____ bright

(h) said the _____

(i) _____ expensive

(j) I can't _____

(k) with the _____

(l) tried it _____

Put it to work

1. Study the sizes which follow. Measure your feet and your body, and figure out about what size you are. See the chart on the following page.

2. Go to a store and try on shoes or clothes. See if your sizes were right.

3. Write a conversation about trying on something that doesn't fit. 1 is a salesman and 2 is a customer.

SIZES

Shoes—Women

	American Size	Measurement of foot
Length:	6	9" long
	6½	
	7	
	7½	9½" long
	8	
	8½	10" long
	9	
	9½	

Width:	AAA	Very narrow
	AA	
	A	Narrow
	B	Medium
	C	
	D	Wide

Shoes—Men

	American Size	Measurement of foot
Length:	8½	
	9½	10½" long
	10	
	10½	
	11	11" long
	11½	
	12	
	12½	11½" long

Women's Blouses	(by bust measurement in inches)
30	
32	Small
34	
36	Medium
38	
40	Large

Men's Shirts	(by neck size, in inches)
14	
14½	Small
15	
15½	Medium
16	
16½	Large

180

Women's Dresses and Pants

(Difficult to give exact sizes)
Dresses come in:
Petite (for very small women 4'5" to
    5'2")
Junior (for slim women; younger
    styles)
Women's (for medium figured women)
Misses (larger in hips than Juniors)
Half-sizes (larger—especially in hips
    —than Women's, may also be
    shorter)

Men's Pants (by waist and leg measurement)

Waist Size	Length of Leg	Size	
29	29	29	29
29	30	29	30
29	31	29	31
30	28	30	28
30	29	30	29
30	30	30	30

Sizes		
3		
4	Very small	
5		
6		
7	Small (e.g., bust 34",	
8	waist 25", hip 35")	
9		
10		
11	Medium (about 36,	
12	28, 38)	
13		
14		
15	Large (38, 30, 42	
16	5'6" tall)	
17		
18	Very large	

Men's Suits, Sport Coats
(chest measurement in inches)
38
40
42
44
46

My sizes are about:

(a) Shoes _____

(b) Blouse or shirt _____

(c) Pants _____

(d) Suit/dress _____

Part 2

Conversation

1: Those are a perfect fit, sir.
2: Well, I guess so, but I don't like this synthetic fabric.
1: Oh, but it washes very well and doesn't need ironing.
2: Yes, but it's uncomfortable in hot weather; so I think I'll take the cotton ones.

Pronunciation

sh and *ch* sounds

washes	exchange	wish
watches	should	witch
match	push	official
admission	toothbrush	check

Sentences:

1. I wish I could exchange these pants.
2. They don't match my shirt.
3. She always washes her toothbrush.
4. I need to cash a check.
5. That official is looking at his watch.

Vocabulary and Idiom Notes

A good (perfect) fit = the right size
I guess so = unsure agreement
Synthetic = man-made; not natural
Fabric = cloth, material used for clothes
Cotton = a natural fabric made from a plant

Structures and functions

Explanation: Often we refer to something we can see or that we have already talked about by using a pronoun. Notice in the conversation that the first speaker uses *"those"* to refer to slacks (see picture) and the second speaker refers to "the cotton *ones.*" Also, both speakers use the pronoun *"it"* to refer to "synthetic fabric" which the second speaker talks about in line 2.

Instruction: Read the following paragraph and find what the italicized pronouns refer to. Sometimes they will refer forward and sometimes back.

These are some of my opinions about living in the city: First of all the people here are very friendly. *They* stop and give you directions when you are lost, and *they* chat with you on buses and subway trains. *It* is cold in the winter, but at other times the weather is very pleasant. Houses are expensive, but I found a cheap *one* in the suburbs. There is always lots to do in the evening. Restaurants are open late, and *those* on the west side often have a great view of the ocean. The subway system is a bit slow, but *it* stretches from one end of town to the other and the mayor is trying to raise money to improve *it*. *She* added an extra ½ percent to the sales tax.

FOCUS: Arguing

Explanation: You can argue and still be polite. In the example below notice how the salesman and the customer argue about the clothes. One agrees with the other, but adds a different idea using "but."

Example: 1: Those are a perfect fit.
          2: I guess so, but I don't like the color.
             (agree)   (disagree)

Instruction: Finish these arguments, using *but* and a disagreement or contradiction.

(a) 1: That's a very pretty sweater.

     2: I guess so, but _____

(b) 1: That turkey was delicious.

     2: Yes, but _____

(c) 1: This brand is very expensive.

     2: Yes, but _____

(d) 1: I don't like my job at the garage.

     2: _____

(e) 1: I had to wait 50 minutes at the dentist.

     2: Too bad, but _____

183

Instruction: Now finish these arguments which start with a contradiction and finish with another opinion.

Example: 1: I like the color of his jacket.
2: I don't, but I like the style.

(a) 1: I think it's too hot in this room.

2: I don't, but _____

(b) 1: It's too expensive _____

2: No it isn't, but _____

(c) 1: She's a great actress.

2: I don't agree, but _____

What do you hear?

1. The teacher will read the passage *Buying a Suit* again. Which form of the verb did you hear?

(a)	decide	decided	deciding
(b)	buys	buyed	buy
(c)	didn't like	don't like	didn't liked
(d)	this fit	this fitted	this fits
(e)	had given	has given	gave
(f)	I can afford	I can't afford	I afforded
(g)	buyed it	bought it	bought it

2. Fill in the blanks from memory.

I _____ decided my suit was worn _____ and _____ I went

_____ Tracy's _____ buy another _____ . There were some

suits on _____ but, unfortunately, I didn't _____ any of them. I tried

on a _____ one from their cheapest line, but it _____ fit me very

_____ . It was the only _____ I liked. The _____ were all too

_____ . "This _____ you perfectly," said the salesman, _____

he had given me the most expensive _____ in the store to _____ .

"It does," I answered, "but I'm _____ I can't afford it. How much is

the charcoal _____ one with the cuffs?"

"That's _____ ."

I tried it on and bought it.

184

Put it to work

1. Study the fabric types which follow. Do you know what they feel like? Discuss their good and bad qualities, for example:

Why are synthetic fabrics popular?
Why do some people prefer cotton to synthetics?
What kind of fabrics are made in your country?

Synthetic fabrics	Natural fabrics
nylon	cotton
dacron	wool
polyester	silk

2. Here are some tags that you might find in clothes. Study the vocabulary, and pay attention to the tags when you shop. Guess what type of clothing each one is.

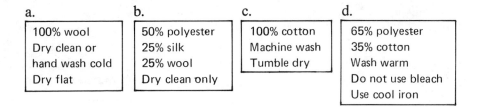

a.
```
100% wool
Dry clean or
hand wash cold
Dry flat
```

b.
```
50% polyester
25% silk
25% wool
Dry clean only
```

c.
```
100% cotton
Machine wash
Tumble dry
```

d.
```
65% polyester
35% cotton
Wash warm
Do not use bleach
Use cool iron
```

What will happen if you wash item *b*?
What will happen if you hang up item *a* when it is wet?
What will happen if you iron item *d* with a hot iron?
Which item will need the most ironing?

Part 3

Conversation

1: Excuse me. I bought this sweater last week, and I want to return it.
2: Well, we don't give refunds, but you can exchange it.
1: The other girl told me I could get my money back.
2: I'm sorry. She wasn't supposed to say that.
1: Maybe I should speak to the manager.

185

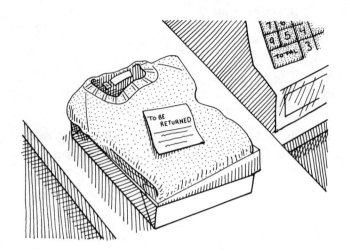

Pronunciation

Supposed to ⟶ sposta

Read:

(a)   She wasn't supposed to say that.
(b)   You weren't supposed to talk.
(c)   The students were supposed to listen.

Vocabulary and Idiom Notes

To return something = to take a thing back to the store and get your money
Refund = the money which is given back
To exchange = to change one thing for another
Wasn't supposed to = shouldn't have
Manager = boss of a store

Structures and functions

FOCUS: *Supposed to*

Explanation: In the past tense, this means about the same as *should have,* as studied in Topic 10. It indicates that something was expected, but it didn't happen.

Instruction: 1.   Use *was/were supposed to* to make sentences out of these two sets of words, as in the following examples:

Plane; 7.00
The plane was supposed to arrive at 10:05.

(a)   My brother; noon

_____

(b)   The teacher; 8:05

_____

(c)   I; last week

_____

(d)   My children; last summer

_____

186

(e)   The employees; last May

_____

2.   Now tell some things you were supposed to do (but you didn't) this morning, yesterday, last week, last year.

_____

_____

_____

_____

FOCUS: *Supposed to* (negative)

Explanation: This indicates that a person did something wrong.

Example: 1:   The girl said I could get a refund, but she was wrong.
          2:   She wasn't supposed to say that.

Instruction: Add a sentence to each one below, using *not supposed to*.

(a)   The children ate all the cake.

_____

(b)   I just washed the floor, and you have dirty feet.

_____

(c)   He turned on the TV. His father was asleep.

_____

(d)   The bank opens at 10:00, but the people pushed the door open at 9:50.

_____

(e)   Tell something you were supposed to do, but you didn't.

_____

What do you hear?

Listen to the passage *An Escaped Criminal*. Take notes; that is, write down as much of the description of the man and woman as you can.

Man: Woman:

_____   _____

_____   _____

_____   _____

_____   _____

Part 4

Conversation

1: Hello, I'm Mrs. Braffett. I'm the manager. May I help you?
2: Yes. One sales clerk told me I could get a refund, and the other one said I couldn't.
1: Well, we don't usually give refunds. We'd prefer to exchange the merchandise.
2: But I don't want to exchange this. There isn't anything else I like.
1: I see. Well, since someone promised you a refund, I'll OK it this time.

Vocabulary and Idiom Notes

To prefer = to like better
Merchandise = things sold in a store
To OK something = to give permission (usually done by the boss)

Structures and functions

FOCUS: Omitting *that* in reported speech

Explanation: In Topic 7, you studied reported speech with *that*. In conversation we often say this kind of sentence without *that*.

Example: The man told me that I could get a job. (with *that*)
The man told me I could get a job. (without *that*)

Instruction: 1. Practice saying these sentences without *that*.

(a)   The clerk told me *that* I could get a refund.

(b) My brother told me that he didn't like anything in the store.

_____

(c) I told him that I wanted a raise.

_____

(d) Sarah told him that she couldn't work on Sundays.

_____

(e) (Tell something that someone told you.)

_____

2. Now mention some things the teacher or other people have told you. Use sentences without *that,* as in the following example:

The teacher told us we could leave early.

(a) _____

(b) _____

(c) _____

FOCUS: Insisting with *but*

Explanation: In Part 1 you practiced arguing politely using *but.* Now use it again to get what you want.

Example: 1:   We can't give refunds.
           2:   But the other clerk said you could.

Instruction: Practice arguing or insisting. Work in pairs.

(a) 1:   These are not on sale.

    2:   But _____

(b) 1:   The store is closed.

    2:   _____

(c) 1:   I'm sorry. I can't fix your car today.

    2:   _____

(d) 1:   Mr. Smith is busy now.

    2:   _____

(e) 1:   Dr. Bennet didn't leave you a message.

    2:   _____

189

(f)   1:   These fit you perfectly, sir.

      2:   _____

(g)   1:   We can't go; it's raining.

      2:   _____

(h)   1:   That TV is too expensive.

      2:   _____

(i)   1:   I'm sorry. You're too late. You've missed the plane.

      2:   _____

(j)   1:   Mr. Smith is busy now.

      2:   _____

**What
do you hear?**

Write a brief description of the man and the woman in the dictation passage, using your notes from Part 3.

_____

_____

_____

_____

Put it to work

1.   The teacher will ask different members of the class to read out some of their clothing sizes. Take notes as they give them. After about five to ten people have given information, go back and check your comprehension.

2.   Look at the clothing ads which follow. Study the vocabulary. Make up a conversation in which you ask a salesperson about one of the articles of clothing, or one in which you have bought something and you want to return it. Work in pairs.

     1:   Excuse me. Where are the shorts that are on sale?

     2:   _____

     1:   _____

TODDLERS' SUMMER TOPS
AND SHORTS

1.99 EA.

knee-length khaki shorts

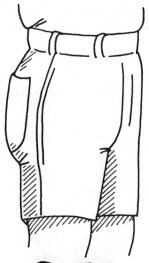

3.79

Women's zip-front cotton
corduroy jacket
Juniors 5–13

12.⁹⁹

Special
support-cup
bras 32AA
to 36C only

2.²⁵

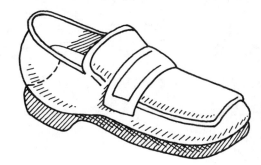

COMFY SOFT
Men's sporty slip-ons
sizes 9 1/2 to 12

15.⁷⁹

Thick,
absorbant
Striped athletic
SOCKS

99¢

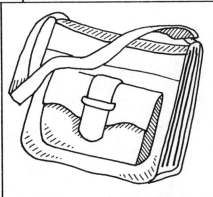

ASSORTED HANDBAGS,
RAINBOW OF COLORS
Your choice, only

11.⁸⁸

Ladies'
Slim jeans,
cuffed or
plain leg
Pocket Decals

9.⁹⁹

TOPIC 12

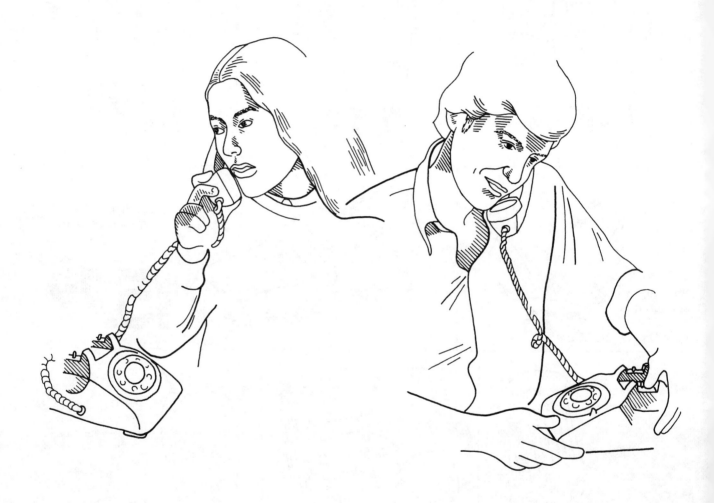

On the Phone:
Problems with Utilities

Part 1

Conversation

(a) 1: Hello. Is Cindy there?
    2: Sure. Just a minute.

(b) 1: Hello. Is Bill there?
    2: No, he isn't. Can I take a message?
    1: No, thanks. I'll call back later.

(c) 1: Hello, Jim. How's it going, man?
    2: Pardon me? What number are you calling?
    1: Uh-oh. Isn't this the Hook residence?
    2: No. You must have the wrong number.
    1: Oh. Sorry to disturb you.

Pronunciation

Practice saying conversation (c) with correct intonation. In line 1, sound friendly; in line 2, sound confused; in line 3, sound sorry.

Vocabulary and Idiom Notes

How's it going? = How are you? (informal)
Residence = home, house
Disturb = bother

Structures and functions

FOCUS: Greetings

Instruction: Name all the ways you remember to greet someone. Tell who you could say them to; then practice saying them naturally, as in the following example:

How's it going, man?   (to a good friend)

(a) _____   _____

(b) _____   _____

(c) _____   _____

(d) _____   _____

(e) _____   _____

(f) _____   _____

(g) _____   _____

FOCUS: Correcting a mistaken call

Explanation: When you answer the telephone and someone asks for a person who does not live in your house, say:

Example: What number are you calling?
  or: I think you have the wrong number.
  or: Sorry. There's no one here by that name.

Instruction: Make up some conversations involving wrong numbers. Work in pairs. Here is an example using one of the alternatives.

Example: 1:   Hello, is Sue there?
            2:   I think you have the wrong number.
            1:   Oh, sorry to bother you.

(a)   1:   _____

      2:   _____

      1:   _____

(b)   1:   _____

      2:   _____

      1:   _____

(c)   1:   _____

      2:   _____

      1:   _____

194

What do you hear?

1. The teacher will read the passage *Using the Phone*. What form of the verb did you hear?

   (a) was living   have lived   have been living
   (b) figured   have figured   has figured
   (c) saves   saved   has saved
   (d) need   needed   needing
   (e) making   have made   can make

2. The teacher will read the passage again. Listen carefully, then list all things the speaker says that you can do on the telephone.

   _____

   _____

   _____

   _____

   _____

Put it to work

1. Discuss these procedures; then do the activities at home.

   (a) Call local information (411), and ask for a telephone number.

   (b) Call long distance information, and ask for a number. Dial 1-area code-555-1212.

   (c) Find out and call the numbers for (you won't have to talk because a recorded conversation will play)

   Time _____

   Weather _____

   Dial-a-story _____

2. Look up these local places in your telephone directory and write the numbers down:

	Name	Number
(a) A department store	_____	_____
(b) A book store	_____	_____
(c) The gas company	_____	_____
(d) The telephone company	_____	_____
(e) A travel agent	_____	_____

Part 2

Conversation

1: Hello, operator? I've been calling the water company for several hours and getting a busy signal.

2: Hold on. I'll try it for you. What's the number?

1: It's area code (290) 444-7017.

2: The phone's off the hook.

1: No wonder I couldn't get them!

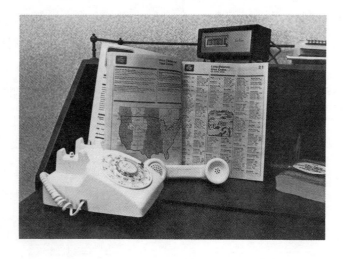

Pronunciation

Practice saying phone numbers clearly. Think about the sounds you have studied.

Go back to Topic 4 and practice ordinal numbers. Concentrate on the difficult ones like *third* and *first*. Make clear distinctions between pairs like 18th-80th, 16th-60th, etc.

Vocabulary and Idiom Notes

Several = many
A busy signal = intermittent buzzing noise; usually means the person at the other end is using the phone
Area code = a three-digit number for different areas of the country
No wonder! = now I understand why!
To get someone = to reach or speak to him

Structures and functions

FOCUS: Present perfect progressive

Explanation: In Topics 3, 4, 6, 7, and 9, you studied the present perfect, using *have/has* plus past participle. Another way to express almost the same idea is to use the progressive form with *have/has* plus *been* plus present participle. Progressive is better than regular present perfect when the action has continued without stopping.

Example: I have been working here for six months =
I have worked here for six months.

Instruction: 1. Complete the conversations using a present perfect progressive form, as in the following example:

1:   Why are you so tired?
2:   I have been running for 20 minutes.

    (a) 1:   Why is he so dirty?

          2:   _____

    (b) 1:   Why are your eyes red?

          2:   _____

    (c) 1:   Why are you in the office?

          2:   _____

    (d) 1:   Why does your hand hurt?

          2:   _____

    (e) 1:   Why is the sugar on the table?

          2:   _____

2.   Tell the class about your home, your work, your hobbies, your studies, etc. Use present perfect progressive when possible.

Example: I have been living in Seattle for two years.

_____

_____

_____

What do you say?

You have to make a telephone call in the following situations. Form a polite way of saying what you need to say in each instance:

(a) Calling up to make an appointment for a job interview.

(b) Calling up to say that you are unable to attend a party.

(c) Calling up to reserve a motel room.

(d) Calling up to inquire about an apartment for rent.

(e) Calling up to apologize for missing a doctor's appointment.

(f) Calling up to invite your boss to dinner.

What do you hear?

Fill in the blanks as the teacher reads the passage *Using the Phone*.

I've _____ living in the United States for _____ a year now, and I've

_____ figured out that you can do almost everything _____ telephone.

Usually _____ calls are free; so it saves to call _____ stores to see if they

have what you _____ before you go there. Most _____ and hotel chains

have toll-free numbers; so you can make _____ anywhere in the country for

_____ by using the 800 area _____ .

Often you can pay _____ by telephone if you have a _____ card.

You can reserve tickets for _____ , find out the _____ , the time, the

_____ conditions, order meals for delivery, get tourist _____ , and find

out if the _____ is good for skiing.

198

Part 3

Conversation

1: Hello, operator. I'd like to call Houston, Texas.
2: You can dial direct.
1: I know, but I want to call person-to-person and charge it to another number.
2: Give me the name, the number, and the number you're calling from.
1: Oh, just a minute. Would it be cheaper if I called on Sunday?
2: Yes, it's cheaper on weekends and holidays and on weekdays before 8 A.M. and after 6 P.M.
1: Thank you, I think I'll call later.

Structures and functions

FOCUS: Questions in the conditional

Explanation: In Topic 5, you studied the conditional (if I *had* time, I *would* fix it). Now look at questions. Either clause can be first.

Example: Would you go if you had time? =
         If you had time, would you go?

Instruction: Complete these questions, using a clause with "would."

(a) If you had time, would _____ ?

(b) If I called at 11:00, _____ ?

(c) _____ if I came over?

(d) _____ if someone gave you $100?

(e) _____ if you saw an accident?

199

Introducing statements with *I think,* to show uncertainty or intention:

Examples: I think I'll stay home. (intention)
I think it's 10:00. (uncertainty)

Instruction: Tell what you think you (or s/he or they) will do:

(a) After school

_____

(b) When you get a job

_____

(c) At Christmas time

_____

(d) On vacation

_____

(e) In a couple of months

_____

What do you hear?

1. The teacher will read the passage *A Missed Call* twice. Answer the following questions:

(a) Why did the speaker wake up early?

_____

(b) What do you think the call was about?

_____

(c) What was wrong with the telephone?

_____

(d) What was the weather like?

_____

(e) What happened on the way to the pay telephone?

_____

(f) How soon did they fix the telephone?

_____

2. Summarize the passage in two or three sentences.

_____

_____

_____

Put it to work 1. Study the telephone bill which follows, and answer the following questions:

(a) How much is owed? _____

(b) What is the service charge? _____

(c) What are the long distance charges? _____

2. Find out what the codes mean—DE, SN, DN, SE, COLL. Which is cheapest? Most expensive?

```
540-3784        Jan 20            555555--661666-333

PREVIOUS CHARGES AND CREDITS

      BALANCE FROM PREVIOUS BILL    39.36
      PAYMENTS AND ADJUSTMENTS      39.36
      CURRENT DUE                    0.00

CURRENT CHARGES AND PAYMENTS

      MONTHLY SERVICE               14.26
      LONG DISTANCE                 20.96
      TAX                            1.33
                                    36.57

      CHARGES DUE JAN 30                       36.57

   TOTAL DUE                                   36.57

         PATRICK ALLEN
         144 DERBY ST.
         ALICEVELLE
```

```
LONG DISTANCE DETAIL

DATE      TIME          MIN    PLACE CALLED    NUMBER      CHARGE

DEC 5     522P    DN    2      Chicago         111-3345      .43
DEC 6     641P    DN    2      Hillty          344-5565      .37
DEC 8     1142A   SE    1      Milton          788-2344      .19
DEC 10    847P    DN    8      Lymmit          535-3847     1.12
Jan 2     756A    DN    34     Hava Hupa       333-2783    18.85

                                                           20.96


KEY       DN = DIAL NIGHT     SE = STATION EVENING    D = DAY
```

Part 4

Conversation

1: Good morning. Northern Gas and Electric Company.
2: Hello, I had a heater installed three days ago, and it hasn't been working right.
1: We won't be able to check it today, but we'll send someone out on Friday.
2: I hope they'll come in the morning.
1: I'm sorry. They'll probably come between 12 and 5 P.M.

Vocabulary and Idiom Notes

Service department = the part of a business that makes repairs

Probably = there is a very good chance that . . .

Note: (The gas and electric company will often check appliances that don't work at no charge to you.)

Structures and functions

FOCUS: Past tense of causative: *had* x + past participle

Explanation: In Topic 6 you studied *to have* x + past participle. You can report that you caused something to happen earlier, by using *had* + past participles.

Instruction: Make up past tense sentences using *had* + past participle, as in the following example:

Put a heater in.
I had a heater put in.

(a) Fix your car

(b) Polish shoes

_____

(c) Cut hair

_____

(d) Cleaning a coat

_____

(e) Repairing a TV

_____

FOCUS: Present perfect progressive, negative

Instruction: Finish the two-line conversations using a present perfect progressive, negative. Work in pairs, as in the following example:

1: The telephone isn't working.
2: I know. It hasn't been working for a week.

(a) 1: It stopped raining!

     2: I know. It _____

(b) 1: You aren't working any more?

     2: No, _____

(c) 1: Have you stopped playing racquet ball?

     2: Yes, _____

(d) 1: I hope it snows soon.

     2: So do I, I _____ (skiing)

(e) 1: You look tired.

     2: I know, I _____

203

FOCUS: *Hope* and *wish*

Explanation: Remember from Topic 5 that *hope* takes the present tense, or a modal.

Example: I hope they will come at 9:00.
           I hope they can come at 9:00.

Explanation: *Wish* is followed by the conditional.

Example: I wish he *would* come (but he won't).
           I wish I *were* president (but I'm not).

Instruction: 1. Tell the class some things you hope will happen in the future.

(a) _____

(b) _____

(c) _____

(d) _____

(e) _____

2.   Now tell some things you wish were true but aren't true.

(a) _____

(b) _____

(c) _____

(d) _____

(e) _____

What do you say?

The telephone rings, you pick up the receiver, say hello, and hear the following words. Give a suitable response.

(a)   Is that Shakey's Pizza Parlor?

_____

(b)   Hello dear, this is your mother.

_____

(c)   This is Mr. Schultz (your boss). I'm calling to find out why you didn't come to work today.

_____

(d)   This is Mrs. Jones from Brand's department store returning your call. You complained about a broken vacuum cleaner?

_____

(e) My name's Mary Jones, and I'm calling from City Insurance. Do you have any life insurance?

_____

What do you hear?

1. The teacher will read the passage *A Missed Call.* Mark the form of the verb you hear.

(a)	work	wake	woked
(b)	know	new	knew
(c)	she heard	she has heard	she had heard
(d)	realizing	realize	realized
(e)	blow	blew	blews
(f)	was damaging	was damaged	damaged
(g)	would try	did try	had tried
(h)	have missed	did miss	had missed

2. Now write the words that come before and after these:

(a) _____ because _____

(b) _____ very _____

(c) _____ something _____

(d) _____ see _____

(e) _____ pouring _____

(f) _____ got _____

(g) _____ would _____

(h) _____ day _____

(i) _____ too _____

Put it to work

1. Saving energy

(a) List the appliances in your home that use gas.

_____

_____

_____

_____

_____

(b) List the appliances that use electricity.

_____

_____

_____

_____

_____

2. Look at the sample brochure from an electric company on the next page.

3. Suggest ways to save energy and lower your gas and electric bill.

A primer on home insulation

Late summer and early fall are good times to begin improving the insulation in your home, well before winter comes storming in. Insulation is among the conservation measures with the greatest energy-saving potential for many homeowners.

What does insulation do? Basically, it slows down the flow of heat through all of the outside surfaces of the house. This means insulation keeps heat *in* during the winter, and keeps heat *out* during the summer.

Before you shop for insulation or talk with a contractor, here are some basic terms with which you should be familiar.

Blanket insulation: Rolls of fiber glass insulation of varying thicknesses. Used for walls, attic floors, basement ceilings, rafters, and crawl spaces.

Batt insulation: Similar to blankets, except that batts are pre-cut into sections, typically 15 or 23 inches wide and four or eight feet long.

Loose-fill insulation: Loose pieces of cellulose fiber or fiber glass insulation, packaged in bags. Also available in vermiculite or perlite for special applications. Poured in between joists, or blown in by special machine. Used for walls or attic floors.

Rigid board insulation: Stiff boards usually made of polystyrene, urethane, fiber glass, or polyisocyanurate. Glued, screwed, or nailed to a smooth surface. Used for ceilings, walls, and foundations. Commonly used in basements and exterior walls in new construction.

R-value: A measure of the insulating ability of a material. The higher the R-value, the better the material's resistance to heat flow. If a material has an R-value of R-2 per inch, five inches of it will provide a total R-value of 10. In New England, at least R-30 is recommended for attics. For walls, the recommended R-values are R-13 for older homes with four-inch walls and R-19 for new construction with six-inch walls.

Vapor barrier: A waterproof material that prevents the moisture naturally present in the air of a house from seeping into insulation and causing it to lose its insulating ability. Vapor barriers come attached to the insulation or are installed separately.

Ventilation: The circulation of air between the house and the outdoors. Proper attic ventilation is necessary to prevent moisture buildup in well-insulated homes. When insulation is added in a home, additional attic ventilation may be needed.

Quiz, Topics 10 to 12

A. Which one is good English?

1. a. Could you tell me when does the bank open?   (Topic 10, Parts 1, 4)
   b. Could you tell me when the bank opens?
   c. Could you tell me when is the bank opens?

2. a. What does *pretest* mean?   (Topic 10, Part 2)
   b. What means *pretest*?
   c. What is *pretest* meaning?

3.   ④   5   ⑥   7   ⑧   9   ⑩

   a. I circled all two numbers.   (Topic 10, Part 3)
   b. I circled every other number.
   c. I circled each two numbers.

4. a. The robber will be caught by the police.   (Topic 10, Part 3)
   b. The robber will catch by the police.
   c. The robber is catch by the police.

5. a. That shoe don't fits me.   (Topic 11, Part 1)
   b. That shoe doesn't fits me.
   c. That shoe doesn't fit me.

6. 1:   This is a very nice car, sir.   (Topic 11, Part 2)
     2:   a. Yes, but it is a beautiful color.
         b. Yes, but it is too expensive.
         c. Yes, but I think I'll buy it.

7. a. I was supposed to wash the dishes, but I didn't.   (Topic 11, Part 3)
   b. I was supposed wash the dishes, but I didn't.
   c. I wasn't supposed to wash the dishes, but I didn't.

8. a. Since it's raining, we'll stay home.   (Topic 11, Part 4)
   b. Since we'll stay home, it's raining.
   c. Since we'll stay home, because it's raining.

9. a. I have been work here for two years.   (Topic 12, Part 2)
   b. I am working here for two years.
   c. I have been working here for two years.

10. a. If you had a car, will you drive to school?   (Topic 12, Part 3)
    b. If you have a car, would you drive to school?
    c. If you had a car, would you drive to school?

208

B. Finish these conversations.

11. 1: Can you _____ ?

     2: Yes. It arrives at 5:00. (Topic 10, Part 1)

12. 1: Joe was crying. What happened to him?

     2: He was _____ (Topic 10, Part 2)

13. 1: _____ ?

     2: It means "a little piece of paper you can use to get into a movie." (Topic 10, Part 2)

14. 1: It's really hot here.

     2: Yeh, but _____ (Topic 11, Part 2)

15. 1: Does that dress _____ ?

     2: Well, not really. Could I try _____ ? (Topic 11, Part 1)

16. 1: Hello, is Mary there?

     2: Yes, _____ (Topic 12, Part 1)

17. 1: I think you have the wrong number.

     2: _____ (Topic 12, Part 1)

18. 1: Why _____ ?

     2: He has been working hard. (Topic 12, Part 2)

19. 1: If I had time, _____

     2: That's a good idea. (Topic 12, Part 3)

20. 1: I wish _____

     2: So _____ (Topic 12, Part 4)

Appendix 1
Dictation Passages

In the U.S.A.

I came to the United States two years ago. I wanted to study, but I didn't have any money. I looked for a job. It was difficult to find one. Everyone told me to study English. About two weeks later I got a job as a janitor. On Friday I got my first check. I didn't have a bank account, so I went to the bank and opened one.

A Letter

I haven't found a place to live yet. I look in the Want Ads every day, but everything is either too far from downtown or too expensive. My friend found a great place the other day. He's sharing a two-bedroom house with a couple. They pay two-thirds of the rent, and he pays one-third. They have a deck and a nice yard, and they're growing vegetables. I'm hoping to find something soon.

My First Day at Work

Well, I'm going to tell you about my first day at work at Sally's Discount Hardware Store. I got up on time (at seven o'clock), got there at eight, took off my coat, and put on my name tag. The boss asked me to go around and mark down all the prices on TV's. I did that. Then I sat down and called up my wife. I had to tell her to pick me up at five o'clock.

When the doors opened, all the sales tags blew away. I had to put them back quickly. At nine o'clock people began to come in. When the customers bought things, I had to add up the price and the tax. Sometimes I made mistakes, and I had to cross everything out and start again. At five o'clock I was worn out.

The Accident

Yesterday, the 16th, there was a terrible accident at the corner of Market and First. An ambulance hit a motorcycle. Then three cars and a bike ran into them. A lot of people got hurt. I've been a reporter for five years, but I've never seen an accident like that. There must be about 20 people in the hospital now. I'll be able to talk to the doctors later, but I can tell you about some of the injuries now. I counted three broken legs, six broken ribs, and about a hundred other cuts and bruises. Thank God, no one got killed.

Honest John

In Reigate, New York, there used to be a very dishonest auto mechanic named Honest John. He was the only mechanic in Reigate. When someone had a flat tire, he used to say, "Oh, the wheel is damaged; you'll have to buy a new one." If a battery died, he used to say, "Sorry, you'll have to buy a new battery." The sign said that labor cost $25.00 an hour, but he really charged $35.00 an hour. Sometimes the parts he put in were older than the parts he took out. The customers couldn't do anything about it.

One day some investigators from the American Auto Association drove through town. They pulled out a small wire from their engine. Then they went to Honest John's garage. He checked their car and said, "Oh, dear! Your car needs a complete overhaul." A few weeks later, Honest John lost his mechanic's license. Another man bought his garage.

Car Trouble

My new Chevrolet is beautiful! But yesterday I had a blowout when I was driving at 60 miles per hour. A policeman was watching. He said I was going 70 miles per hour, but he didn't give me a ticket. I took the car to the garage, and they told me my tire pressures were too low in the other tires. They were 20 pounds per square inch in the front and 18 psi in the rear. They told me the correct pressure for my car is 27 psi in the front and 24 psi in the rear.

Dear Mom

June 26

Dear Mom,

I put off going to the dentist again. I finally went yesterday after two years. You must be ashamed of me. I was really scared of the shots because I'm allergic to Novocain, as you know. When I came in, the assistant was cleaning up the instruments. They looked like hundreds of sharp knives. Ugh!

After twenty minutes, the dentist came in. I tried to put off having my teeth filled, but she didn't let me get out of it. The X-rays were okay. Although I was nervous, the drill didn't hurt too much. Dr. Gore turned up the stereo, and I could only hear music. I put back my head and relaxed. I listened to about five songs. I suddenly woke up three-quarters of an hour later as someone said, "Your husband is here to pick you up!" What an easy time! The $55.00 dental bill was more painful than the filling.

Love,
Jill

Personal Information

(a) What is your zip code?

(b) What is your age?

(c) Have you been employed before?

(d) How many dependents do you have?

(e) Are you single or married?

(f) How many years of school have you completed?

(g) Did you go to college?

(h) Do you prefer full-time or part-time work?

(i) Have you ever been in jail?

(j) Please print your name.

(k) Please sign your name.

The Corner Store

I had a flat tire, and it took ten minutes to walk to the corner store from my house. I bought a carton of milk, some bread, some cheese, and some bacon. I had to buy a one-liter bottle of cooking oil because they were out of the smaller ones. I wanted some fruit, too. The cherries were riper than the plums, but the peaches looked the best. I asked for two pounds, but the storekeeper gave me a kilo. He told me to change to kilos and grams. Pounds and ounces are out of date. It took me 20 minutes to walk home.

An Invitation

Next Wednesday is July 4th. Chuck and Lily invited me over for a barbecue, but I think I'll go with Philip and Janice to a picnic in the park.

Chuck and Lily are very kind. I spent Thanksgiving with them last year, and they asked me for Christmas, too, but I had to refuse because I went back to Hong Kong.

Susie called me yesterday and invited me to a formal dinner in town. I'd like to go, but I'd have to rent a tuxedo. Maybe I can borrow one from Gene.

American Holidays

1. July 4th is Independence Day.
2. Thanksgiving Day falls on the fourth Thursday in November.
3. Valentine's Day is on February 14th. It is not a holiday.
4. Christmas Day is December 25th.
5. January 1st is New Year's Day.
6. Labor Day is the first Monday in September.
7. Halloween is October 31st. It is not a holiday.
8. Memorial Day is the last Monday in May.

Chocolate Cake

Preheat oven to 350°. Sift 1 ¾ c. flour with 3 t. baking powder, ¼ t. salt, 1 t. cinnamon or nutmeg. Melt 2 oz. chocolate. Add 5 T. boiling water. Beat ½ c. butter and 1 ½ c. sugar. Beat in 3 egg yolks, add the chocolate, add half the flour mixture and ¼ c. milk. Then add the rest of the flour and ¼ c. more milk. Mix well and add 1 t. vanilla. Fold in 3 beaten egg whites. Bake 25–30 minutes.

Buying an Airplane Ticket

"Good morning, I'd like to make a reservation for two to Miami."

"When did you want to leave?"

"Thursday the 25th."

"Round-trip or one-way?"

"One-way."

"O.K. You have two choices: Flight 271 leaves at 7:05 a.m., arriving in New York at 10:26. You connect with Flight 56 departing at 11:14 and arriving in Miami at 1:23. The other is a night flight leaving at 11:29 p.m. and arriving in Miami at 4:06 the next morning. The night fare is cheaper than the day fare."

"O.K., thanks. Please reserve us seats on the night flight."

Instructions, Topic 10, Part 3

(a) Circle every other number.

(b) Underline every other letter.

(c) Circle every third dot.

(d) Draw a circle in every other square.

(e) Mark an X on every fourth triangle.

(f) Put a two-digit number on every third line.

(g) Put a check on each line.

(h) Write down every other number from one to nine.

(i) Cross out every third month.

(j) Underline the second and fifth days.

The Terrible Vacation

"Have you heard about my terrible vacation?"

"No. What happened?"

"Well. I was invited to go camping, but they forgot to pick me up, and I had to hitchhike to the campsite."

"Oh, no! What else happened?"

"Well, their tent was stolen, and we had to sleep outside in the rain."

"That's awful!"

"That's not all. We were supposed to go fishing, but their boat was sunk during the night."

"Oh, dear. What else happened?"

"I don't know. I came home on the bus the next day."

Buying a Suit

I finally decided my suit was worn out, and yesterday I went to Tracy's to buy another one. There were some suits on sale, but, unfortunately, I didn't like any of them. I tried on a tan one from their cheapest line, but it didn't fit me very well. It was the only color I liked. The others were all too bright. "This fits you perfectly," said the salesman, after he had given me the most expensive suit in the store to try on.

"It does," I answered, "but I'm afraid I can't afford it. How much is the charcoal gray one with the cuffs?"

"That's $159.95."

I tried it on and bought it.

213

An Escaped Convict

Yesterday the police interviewed me. They are looking for an escaped criminal who was in my hometown. His description was: black hair, height: 6'1", weight 176 pounds, age: 32, race: Caucasian. Since he had stolen some clothes, they also had details about what he was wearing: tennis shoes, size 11; a black T-shirt, extra large; jeans, 34 waist, 32 leg; denim jacket, size 42, and a black beret, size 7½. He is wanted for murder. He might be traveling with a woman with dark hair, 5 feet 4 inches tall, 112 pounds, age: 26. She was wearing cutoffs, a white T-shirt, flat shoes, and a blue sweater over her shoulders.

Using the Phone

I've been living in the United States for nearly a year now, and I've just figured out that you can do almost everything by telephone. Usually local calls are free; so it saves to call up stores to see if they have what you need before you go there. Most airlines and hotel chains have toll-free numbers; so you can make reservations anywhere in the country for nothing by using the 800 area code.

Often, you can pay bills by telephone if you have a credit card. You can reserve tickets for shows, find out the weather, the time, the traffic conditions, order meals for delivery, get tourist information, and find out if the snow is good for skiing.

A Missed Call

Today was a disaster, and all because of the telephone. I woke up at 6 a.m. because I was expecting a very important telephone call from abroad. By seven-thirty I knew something was wrong. I tried to call Mary to see if she had heard anything, but I couldn't get a dial tone; so I realized my telephone was out of order. It was pouring rain; so I put on my raincoat and boots, and walked down the street to the pay phone. The wind blew my umbrella inside out, and I got soaked. The telephone people said that a line was damaged by the storm, but they would try to fix it right away. I waited all day until they made the repairs, but by then it was too late, and I had missed a day's work for nothing.

Appendix 2
Numbers

1	one	1st	first
2	two	2nd	second
3	three	3rd	third
4	four	4th	fourth
5	five	5th	fifth*
6	six	6th	sixth
7	seven	7th	seventh
8	eight	8th	eighth*
9	nine	9th	ninth*
10	ten	10th	tenth
11	eleven	11th	eleventh
12	twelve	12th	twelfth*
13	thirteen	13th	thirteenth
14	fourteen	14th	fourteenth
15	fifteen	15th	fifteenth
16	sixteen	16th	sixteenth
17	seventeen	17th	seventeenth
18	eighteen	18th	eighteenth
19	nineteen	19th	nineteenth
20	twenty	20th	twentieth*
21	twenty-one	21st	twenty-first
22	twenty-two	22nd	twenty-second
23	twenty-three	23rd	twenty-third
24	twenty-four	24th	twenty-fourth
25	twenty-five	25th	twenty-fifth
26	twenty-six	26th	twenty-sixth
27	twenty-seven	27th	twenty-seventh
28	twenty-eight	28th	twenty-eighth
29	twenty-nine	29th	twenty-ninth*
30	thirty	30th	thirtieth*
40	forty*	40th	fortieth*
50	fifty*	50th	fiftieth*
60	sixty	60th	sixtieth*
70	seventy	70th	seventieth*
80	eighty	80th	eightieth*
90	ninety	90th	ninetieth*
100	one hundred	100th	one hundredth
1,000	one thousand	1,000th	one thousandth
2,000	two thousand	2,000th	two thousandth

*Notice the spelling changes.

215

Appendix 3
Irregular Verbs

I. Past Tense = Past Participle

bend	bent	bent
bleed	bled	bled
bring	brought	brought
build	built	built
buy	bought	bought
catch	caught	caught
cost	cost	cost
cut	cut	cut
dig	dug	dug
feed	fed	fed
feel	felt	felt
fight	fought	fought
find	found	found
fit	fit	fit
hang	hung	hung
had	had	had
hear	heard	heard
hit	hit	hit
hold	held	held
hurt	hurt	hurt
keep	kept	kept
lay	laid	laid
lead	led	led
leave	left	left
let	let	let
lose	lost	lost
make	made	made
mean	meant	meant
meet	met	met
pay	paid	paid
put	put	put
quit	quit	quit
read	read	read
say	said	said
sell	sold	sold
send	sent	sent
set	set	set

shut	shut	shut
sit	sat	sat
sleep	slept	slept
spend	spent	spent
spread	spread	spread
stand	stood	stood
sweep	swept	swept
teach	taught	taught
tell	told	told
win	won	won
wind	wound	wound

II. Past Tense is different from past participle

A. Alphabetical Order

begin	began	begun
bite	bit	bitten
blow	blew	blown
break	broke	broken
choose	chose	chosen
come	came	come
do	did	done
draw	drew	drawn
drink	drank	drunk
drive	drove	driven
eat	ate	eaten
fall	fell	fallen
fly	flew	flown
freeze	froze	frozen
get	got	gotten
give	gave	given
go	went	gone
grow	grew	grown
hide	hid	hidden
know	knew	known
ride	rode	ridden
ring	rang	rung
run	ran	run
see	saw	seen
shake	shook	shaken
shrink	shrank	shrunk
sink	sank	sunk
sing	sang	sung
speak	spoke	spoken
steal	stole	stolen
swim	swam	swum
take	took	taken
tear	tore	torn
throw	threw	thrown

wake up	woke up	woken/wakened
wear	wore	worn
write	wrote	written

B.   Grouped by:

en participle

bite	bit	bitten
break	broke	broken
choose	chose	chosen
drive	drove	driven
fall	fell	fallen
freeze	froze	frozen
get	got	gotten
give	gave	given
hide	hid	hidden
ride	rode	ridden
shake	shook	shaken
speak	spoke	spoken
steal	stole	stolen
take	took	taken
wake	woke	woken
write	wrote	written

-n participle

blow	blew	blown
draw	drew	drawn
fly	flew	flown
grow	grew	grown
know	knew	known
see	saw	seen
tear	tore	torn
throw	threw	thrown
wear	wore	worn

present = participle

come	came	come
run	ran	run

present *i*—past *a*—participle *u*

drink	drank	drunk
ring	rang	run
shrink	shrank	shrunk
sink	sank	sunk
sing	sang	sung
swim	swam	swum

other

do	did	done
go	went	gone
is	was/were	been

218

Appendix 4
Abbreviations

I. Want Ads

A. Apartments

AEK	all electric kitchen
agt	agent
apt	apartment
avail	available
ba	bath
bldg	building
br	bedroom
condo	condominium
cpt	carpet
drp	drapes
elev	elevator
exc	excellent
flrs	floors
fplc	fireplace
frig	refrigerator
gar	garage
gdn	garden
hdwd	hardwood floors
inc/incl	includes
kch	kitchen
lg	large
mo	month
nr	near
nudec	newly decorated
pd	paid
refs	references
rm	room
sgl	single
spec	special
stu	studio
trans	transportation
util	utilities
W/D	washer/dryer
vw	view
wk	week
w/w	wall to wall
yd	yard

B. Help Wanted (Jobs)

acctg	accounting
adm	administration
appt	appointment
asst	assistant
avail	available
bi-ling	bilingual
bkgd	background
co	company
comm	commission
cple	couple
dep	depends
educ	education
exc/excl	excellent
exper	experience
ext	extension
gd	good
hrs	hours
immed	immediate
ins/insur	insurance
lic	license
m/f	male/female
mech	mechanic
med	medical
mgmt	management
mgr	manager
min	minimum
mo	month
nat'l	national
nec	necessary
nego	negotiable
ofc	office
oppty	opportunity
pref	preferred
refs	references
req/req'd	required
S/H	shorthand
sal	salary
supv.	supervisor (boss)
w	with
wpm	words per minute
yr	year
yrs	years

C. Auto (cars)

a c/air	air conditioning
AM/FM	good radio (with frequency (F) and amplitude (A) modulation)
AT	automatic transmission

220

auto	automatic
beaut	beautiful
blk	black
CAD	Cadillac
cass	cassette deck
CHEV/CHEVY	Chevrolet
cond	condition
conv	convertible
cyl	cylinders
dr	drive
equip	equipment
eve	evenings
exc	excellent
int	interior
K mi.	thousand miles
lo	low
met	metallic
MERC	Mercury
mi	miles
mint	mint condition (perfect)
MUST	Mustang
nu	new
ofr	offer
OLDS	Oldsmobile
pass	passenger
PB	Power brakes
PLYM	Plymouth
PONT	Pontiac
PS	Power steering
reb/rblt	rebuilt
pwr	power
snrf	sunroof
spd	speed
ster	steering
V-6/V-8	6-cylinder, 8-cylinder (engine size)
wgn	wagon (station wagon)

II. Acronyms and Initials

A. General

A.D.	Anno Domini (years after Christ was born)
B.C.	Before Christ
C.I.A.	Central Intelligence Agency (spies)
F.B.I.	Federal Bureau of Investigation (U.S. government police)
C.B.S.	Columbia Broadcasting Company
N.B.C.	National Broadcasting Company (TV networks)
A.B.C.	American Broadcasting Company

221

G.E.	General Electric	
G.M.	General Motors	
I.B.M.	International Business Machines	(Big companies)
I.T.T.	International Telephone and Telegraph	
I.D.	Identification	
I.O.U.	I owe you	
I.Q.	Intelligence quotient	
M.P.H.	Miles per hour	
N.A.S.A.	National Aeronautics and Space Administration	
N.	North	
S.	South	
E.	East	(directions: also N.W., N.E., S.W., S.E.)
W.	West	
A.M.	Ante meridian (morning)	
P.M.	Post meridian (afternoon)	
P.S.	Post script (used to add another thought at the end of a letter)	
P.T.A.	Parent-Teacher Association (a group at schools)	
R.P.M.	Revolutions per minute (for describing car engines)	
R.S.V.P.	Répondez s'il vous plait (please answer)	
S.O.S.	Help!	
U.N.	United Nations	
U.S.A.	United States of America	
U.S.S.R.	Union of Soviet Socialist Republics (Russia)	

B. Degrees

A.A.	Associate of arts (two-year college)	
A.B./B.A.	Bachelor of arts	(four-year college)
B.S.	Bachelor of science	
M.A.	Master of arts	
M.S.	Master of sciences	
M.B.A.	Master of business administration	
L.L.B.	Law degree	
Ph.D.	Doctor of philosophy	
L.V.N.	Licensed vocational nurse	
R.N.	Registered nurse	
D.D.S.	Dentist	
M.D.	Medical doctor	

Appendix 5
Weights and Measures

Conversion Scales

Linear

    1 foot = 0.3048 meter
    1 centimeter = 0.3937 inch
    1 mile = 1.609 kilometers
    1 kilometer = 0.621 miles
    1 yard = 0.9144 meter
    1 meter = 1.904 yards or 39.37 inches

Weight

    1 gram = 0.035 ounce (oz)
    1 kilogram = 2.205 pounds (lb)
    1 ounce = 31.1 grams

Volume

    1 ounce = 29.573 milliliters
    1 pint (dry) = 0.551 liter
    1 pint (liquid) = 0.946 liter
    1 liter = 1.057 liquid quart
    1 quart (liquid) = 0.946 liter
    1 gallon = 3.785 liters

Temperature

    (To convert Fahrenheit to Celsius, subtract 32, multiply by 5, and divide by 9.)
    $0°C. = 32°F.$ (freezing)
    $100°C. = 212°F.$ (boiling)

Appendix 6
Answers to "What Do You Say?"

Answers	Clues
Topic 1, Part 2	
(a)	Polite, formal, but expecting service (I'd like). "Excuse me" is used for calling attention.
(b)	Polite, to a known person (Mr. Wong).
(c)	Very familiar (hey), announcing the intention to borrow the book rather than asking.
(d)	Begging, stating desire rather than asking.
(e)	Direct order, only for authority figure (or robber).

Topic 1, Part 3

(a)	1, possibly 4	Polite, but to a well-known person (first name).
(b)	3	Use of "sir" indicates serving person.
(c)	2 (or 5)	Darling is only for loved ones.
(d)	4, possibly 1	Polite, but informal
(e)	5	Direct order, with caution to be careful, typical "mother-ese."

Topic 2, Part 2

(a)	2	"Darling," "lovely" are usually used by women.
(b)	3	Men often like cars; a garage is important. Home offices may be associated with men, although women often use them, too. (Note, native speakers recognize this as men's language, but customs are changing. It may be considered "sexist" to talk about men's and women's language.)
(c)	4	Use of "my own bedroom" indicates that a separate room is special. Nearness to school indicates that the person is a student.
(d)	1	Number of details, such as size and type of kitchen.

Topic 2, Part 4

(a)	2	"While you . . ." indicates that the person is just arriving.
(b)	1	Concern with work.
(c)	3	"Are you . . . and do you . . ." is a courtroom expression or "formula."
(d)	4	Giving person information (I'm from . . .)
(e)	5	Just labels, not conversation

Answer	Clues

Topic 4, Part 2

(a)

Family member, probably an adult. "Poor thing "is familiar. "Have you taken . . ." indicates an adult who could take medicine without help.

(b) 2=child
1=mother

"Tummy" is baby talk for stomach.
"Sweetheart" is familiar. "Let's find . . ." is reassuring, promising help.

(c) 1=doctor
2=patient

"Mrs. Garcia" is formal. ". . . to go home" indicates that it takes place in a hospital and that 1 will decide when 2 can go home.

Topic 5, Part 1

(a) 3   "Sir" indicates respect and formal relationship.

(b) 2   Technical language; a nonmechanic would not understand ("jets," "idle screw").

(c) 1   "Bob" indicates friendliness, informality.

(d) 4   Refers to his dad

(e) 5   Speaker repeats the same thing three different ways, making it simpler ("broken," "no good," "finished").

Topic 5, Part 3

(a) "Pardon me" is a formal way of calling attention; "Dad" is informal.

(b) "Get over here" is a direct order, not very polite. "Could you . . ." is very polite.

(c) "I want you to . . ." is a command by a boss. He would not offer to get coffee for the same employee.

Topic 6, Part 2

(a) 3   "Mrs. Evans" is very polite. Sounds like a boss. "It won't happen again" is an adult-like promise.

(b) 2   "Honey" is familiar. Asking about the wait is polite and also friendly.

(c) 4   Denying fault is typical of children. "You know that" is not polite. (This child may be punished for rudeness.)

(d) 1   It is customary for a child to take a note to the teacher if he is late or absent.

Topic 7, Part 2

(a) 3   Request for service "I'd like . . . ," asking about more than one job.

(b) 2   "Hey" and "why don't you" are familiar.

(c) 4   Polite request about one job. "You have . . ." indicated that the speaker is addressing the employer.

(d) 1   Direct order. "Be quiet" is probably from a parent to a child. If not, it is quite rude.

Answer	Clues
Topic 7, Part 3	

(a)

Not polite enough

(b)

Rude and not clear what you want

(c)

Too direct

(d) Good

Polite, but strong request. "I would like . . ." is stronger than "Can I . . ."

(e)

Polite, but not clear what you want. Most people who have an office see people only by appointment.

(f)

You need the title "Mr." when referring to a possible employer.

Topic 8, Part 2

1   (c)
2   (b)
3   (a)
4   (d)

Topic 8, Part 4

(a) Excuse me, could you lend me $10. I'll pay you back tomorrow.
(b) Hey, Joe, can I borrow $10? I'm a little short today.
(c) Hey, Gimme ten, will you? I know you've got plenty.
(d) All right, you give me that $10 now or else you're in trouble.

Topic 10, Part 2

(a) 2

Polite ". . . sir"; mentions "in this country."

(b) 1

Formal ". . . did you want." Exact time: "the morning of the 25th."

(c) 5

Friendly, ". . . can you stay . . ." "if you can stand it" is a joke.

(d) 3

Request to check on a flight indicates travel agent or airline.

(e) 4

Shows concern for how much time they can spend together "when do you have to go," "not until . . ."

Topic 12, Part 2

(a) Hello, my name is Jose Gonzales. I'm calling because I would like to make an appointment with Mrs. Carter.
(b) Hello, John? Hi, this is Sandy. Thanks for the invitation to your party. It's too bad, but we can't make it that day. We have to go to a wedding.
(c) Yes, I'd like to make a reservation for a double room on the night of the 26th.
(d) I'm calling about the apartment you advertised. Is it still available?
(e) This is Dan Lee. I'm afraid I missed my appointment with Dr. Yan this morning. I'm sorry I didn't call earlier, but my car was stolen.
(f) Hello, Mr. Wang? This is Paul. I was wondering if you and your wife could come to dinner on Friday, the 6th?

Topic 12, Part 4

(a) No, I'm afraid you have the wrong number.
(b) Hi, mom, how are you?
(c) Oh, thank you for calling. I left a message this morning to say I was sick.
(d) Yes, the first time I used it, the motor overheated.
(e) I'm not interested. Thank you.